Souls Stick Around

A Tale of the Black Hills and Maurice Gibb

Dawnette Owens

This book is dedicated to the family, friends, and fans of Maurice Gibb and to my husband, Rollie.

The following story is fictitious. Although the character of Maurice Gibb is loosely based on Maurice Gibb, the incidences and conversations in the story are the sole imagination of the author.

Chapter 1

A Wednesday morning in the middle of May 2002

THE PHONE RANG at seven in the morning.

"Yes-s-s," I answered, expecting my husband, Nick, to be on the other line.

"Hello, is this Caroline Nichols?" said a voice sporting a British accent.

Hmmm, not too many Brits work as American telemarketers, so I replied in a friendly voice, "Yes, it is."

"Right. I'm Maurice Gibb. I believe you sent a letter inviting me to spend a few days your way. I'm calling to see if you're still up for a visit."

My heart started to beat so loudly I thought I wouldn't be able to hear myself think. Then my defense mechanisms kicked in.

"Okay Nick, you got me. You need me to drop off something on my way to work?"

I heard a chuckle on the other line, unlike Nick's normal laugh.

"Sorry love, this isn't Nick. I really am Maurice."

"Oh my God! You got my letter and you, and you read it!"

"Yes, I pride myself on my reading abilities."

"Oh, uhm, uh, right," I muttered along with a nervous little giggle before I took a deep breath and gathered enough of my senses to answer, "Of course I'm up for a

1

visit. We'd love to have you anytime. When were you thinking of coming?"

"If it's convenient, this weekend."

Without giving it a second thought, I answered, "This weekend would be great." Between pounding heart beats, I added, "Will your wife be joining you?"

"Yvonne will be visiting friends in Denver this weekend, so, no, she won't be accompanying me. But, I have a personal assistant who'll be popping in on us every once and a while."

"That'd be great," I said.

"You haven't had time to check with Nick yet. How about I ring you tonight to confirm this weekend. Will you and the would-be prankster be home at eight?"

"Your time or mine?"

"I completely forgot about the bloody time change," said Maurice. "I apologize for ringing you so early this morning."

"Oh, don't worry about it. I've been up for hours. Eight your time will work."

"Brilliant. I'll ring you then."

I was able to place the phone back on the receiver before I started to freak out.

OH MY GOD—MO GIBB IS COMING TO MY HOUSE.

I have a million things to do before then, including clean the house, give my Golden Retriever a bath, tidy up the yard, buy new furniture, lose ten pounds, and turn myself into an interesting person.

As promised, Maurice called back in the evening. After he and Nick got acquainted, Maurice and I discussed possible activities for the weekend. We also agreed to a couple of guidelines—rid the house of alcohol and keep his visit low key.

I started to give Maurice directions to our house, but he said he didn't need them. He confessed he had his assistant run a low-key security check on us. Well good for him. Plus, we had nothing to hide, except perhaps for Nick's bowling pin lamps.

A MONTH EARLIER I had sent Maurice a letter describing how I rediscovered the Bee Gees' music as a result of buying myself a Christmas present last December when I should have been shopping for legitimate people on my list.

In my first official fan letter, I described how I went to the mall's record store preparing to buy the CD of an artist whose music I hadn't already owned. I considered Nora Jones, Pink, and Eminem before I happened across the "B" section. I picked up *This is Where I Came In* not realizing the Bee Gees had released a new CD. The last recording I could specifically name from the Bee Gees was the *Saturday Night Fever* soundtrack, which I still owned in album form. Without hesitation, I bought *This is Where I Came In*, excited to hear current music from the Brothers Gibb.

My reawakening began when I popped my Christmas present in the car's CD player. By the middle of the first cut, I felt proud that the group that sang some of my favorite songs from the sixties and seventies was still composing and recording music I enjoyed.

Even though heavy snow was falling, I bypassed my driveway forty minutes later, so I could experience the entire CD in one sitting. Once I got home, I searched the Internet to find out what the Bee Gees had been up to since the disco era. I was pleasantly surprised to learn they still remained as busy as they had in the seventies.

Under the guise of another Christmas shopping excursion, I returned to the record store the next day to buy a couple more Bee Gees CDs, both of which impressed me so much I went back for more. After the record stores in the area couldn't keep up with me, I bought more off the Internet. At the time I sent the letter to Maurice, I owned half of the thirty or so Bee Gees CDs available and eagerly anticipated completing my collection.

I would peruse the sleeve of each of my new CDs like I used to do with album covers, but now often with squinted eyes. My extensive sleeve-cover reading revealed that although Maurice sang harmony on most songs, he was also a multi-instrumentalist and typically sang lead on one or two songs per CD.

In my letter to Maurice, I wrote that even though I didn't know much about him personally, I was captivated by his music. I acknowledged Barry and Robin's remarkable voices, but added that whenever I listened to a new Bee Gees CD, I looked forward most to Maurice's lead songs.

I also sheepishly admitted that although I loved the Bee Gees' music in the sixties and seventies, I was one of those people who stopped listening when disco bashing became popular.

Although I knew I was being presumptuous, particularly considering my behavior during the disco era, I invited Maurice to visit me, my husband Nick, and our Golden Retriever at our home in the beautiful Black Hills of South Dakota. As a reference point, I mentioned that Mount Rushmore is located ten minutes from our house.

Of course, I didn't expect Maurice to accept my offer. I didn't even expect to hear back. I sent the letter because it made me feel good to let him know how much his music has made an impact on me.

I TOOK THURSDAY and Friday off from work to get ready for Maurice's visit and to make lists of "must do activities" and "if we can squeeze them in ventures." Every few minutes I pinched myself to make sure I wasn't dreaming. I quit when I realized welts were forming on my skin.

Besides the welts, I'm in my early forties and stand just over five feet. I have naturally curly brunette hair that I wear shoulder length. My most prominent features are my big brown eyes, which some of my friends call "cow eyes." I don't know how flattering the description is, but it's pretty accurate.

Nicholas Nichols has hazel eyes and wavy black hair that's graying at the temples. He's a few inches shy of six feet and possesses one of the nicest physiques this side of the Missouri River, due in part to his job as a forest service worker.

Nick and I live in our dream home—a log house we built ourselves. The front of the striking, two-story house is accentuated by a fireplace chimney made from handsome river rock. Immense floor-to-ceiling windows are located on either side of the chimney.

The main entry is located on the side of the house facing the driveway. A covered porch over the entry connects to a deck that wraps around most of the house.

Once inside the house, the eyes are drawn to the front windows and the fireplace. Besides its beauty, the fireplace provides the main source of heat for our home.

The living room furnishings consist of mismatched furniture and conversation pieces that fit together comfortably, including a keyboard and an acoustic guitar.

Positioned along the far wall are the dining room area and a patio door that leads to a screened-in, heated porch. The small, but efficient, U-shaped kitchen is located on the other side of the patio door. Beyond the kitchen are the master bedroom and bathroom, utility room, guest bathroom, and garage.

The second story is accessible by means of a log stairwell just off the kitchen. The front two-thirds of the second floor are open to below, allowing for the main floor's living area to be viewed from the second floor's landing. Facing the back of the second story, a combination bedroom and office is located to the left, while another bedroom is located on the right. Patio doors on the back walls of both bedrooms lead to a balcony.

The bathroom, positioned between the two bedrooms, lays claim to the second floor's preeminent feature—a glass back wall. The tub and shower are located along the transparent wall, affording bathers a magnificent view of our property and the adjoining forest service land.

The house is located a comfortable walking distance from the main road. If we don't dawdle, my eleven-year-old Golden Retriever, Shelby, and I can make our morning excursion to collect the newspaper in about seven minutes.

Chapter 2

AFTER MUCH PRODDING from me, Nick took Friday afternoon off. I knew I'd be a bundle of nerves until Maurice arrived, so I wanted Nick to bear the brunt of my energy.

I had never been more nervous than I was waiting for Maurice. I peered out the window every few minutes to see if his car was pulling up the driveway. Nick, amused by my behavior, suggested we wait for Maurice on the front porch. To make it look like we were doing more than waiting, we held glasses of iced tea. Nick even drank out of his.

We heard gravel from the driveway crunch beneath tires before we saw the vehicle, a white Range Rover with South Dakota plates. The windows were tinted so we weren't certain it was Maurice. However, since we didn't get too many unexpected visitors, my heart began to pound anxiously.

A few seconds after the vehicle stopped in front of the garage, a slender, bespectacled, bearded man emerged from the passenger door—it was Maurice! He immediately strode over to greet us.

"Hello, I'm Maurice. You must be Caroline."

Maurice shook my hand and gave me a half hug with his left arm.

"And you must be Nick," he said as he shook Nick's hand.

Approaching us was the Range Rover's driver.

"And this is Gordon, my personal assistant. He'll be spending some time with us this weekend, if you don't mind."

Gordon, who was in his early thirties, wore his bleached hair shoulder length and stood a good foot taller than me.

"Nice to meet you Gordon," I said shaking his hand. "We're glad both of you could make it to our little part of the world."

Shelby began to run toward Maurice. As she got closer, she activated her wiggle butt, which caused her to slow down.

"Who is this beautiful creature?" Maurice said as he bent down to pet her.

"This is Shelby. If she bothers you at all, we can put her in her kennel."

"Are you kidding?" answered Maurice. "I love dogs and Goldens are one of my favorite breeds."

Shelby sat in front of Maurice and extended her left paw, which Maurice promptly shook.

"The southpaw's quite the flirt, isn't she," said Maurice.

"She senses you're a dog lover," I said.

"She's smart, too," Maurice said as he straightened up and stroked her head. "You have a fabulous place. Almost like I pictured it."

"Oh, I almost forgot." He sprinted back to the vehicle to retrieve a huge basket of fruit. "This is a gift from my wife, Yvonne, and me. She extends her regrets at not being able to accompany me."

"How thoughtful. Please thank her," I said as Nick carried the basket loaded with oranges, grapefruits, limes, crackers, cheese, and most importantly, chocolate, into the house.

"Come in," I said. "We'll give you a tour of the house before we show off the yard."

"I've never been in a log house before. This will be a treat," Maurice said as he and Gordon stepped in the entryway. Maurice's eyes gravitated toward the front windows and the fireplace.

"How long have you lived here?" Maurice asked.

"Well, we began building it about fifteen years ago," said Nick.

"You built this house?" asked Maurice.

"Before we were married," I said, "Nick lived on the property in a little cabin, which we have since transformed into the garage. After doing a lot of research and scrimping and saving, we were able to start building a couple years after we got married."

"You must have had some help," said Maurice.

"We actually did the majority of the work ourselves," said Nick. "But we resorted to blackmail, kidnapping, and home cooking to get friends to help us with the heavy construction. Surprisingly, some of those people still talk to us."

"How long did it take you?" asked Gordon.

"Ask us when we're through," I said as I led everyone up the stairs. "We still have some detail work left, which honestly may never get done. But it took a little over a year before we were able to move in."

"I know you have reservations at a nearby B&B," I continued, "but you're both more than welcome to stay here. I've made up these two bedrooms in case you change your minds."

Maurice and Gordon made several complimentary remarks as they wandered through the second floor. Maurice opened the small refrigerator in the bathroom and smiled when he spotted the Coke in the upper rack.

"Nice touch," said Maurice. "You're trying to entice us with your hospitality. I'm surprised you haven't cued the deer yet to come wandering across the lawn."

I glanced at my watch before I answered, "They're not scheduled for another ten minutes. Speaking of the lawn, let's head outside. I want to show off Nick's horticultural skills."

As we walked down the stairs, Maurice spotted the keyboard and guitar in the living room.

"So, there's a musician in the family."

"I wish that were the case," I answered. "I'm nothing more than a dabbler. I took piano lessons when I was a teenager. Then a few years ago, Nick bought me the guitar as a Christmas present. I've tinkered with it, but I really don't know how to play. One of these years, though, I'll get back to playing both."

WE WENT OUT the front door just in time to see three deer dart across the lawn.

"I'm impressed," said Maurice. "The deer reported for duty even ahead of schedule. What a beautiful location. Do you mind if I ask how many acres you own?"

"Six," Nick replied. "Plus, the property's surrounded by forest service land. We get to enjoy the adjoining property without having to pay for it. Our piece belonged to my grandparents. When they passed away years ago, my parents inherited it. They turned around and gave me three acres. When Caroline and I got married, we bought the other three from them."

"I married Nick for his land," I said. "But don't tell him."

"I maintain about two acres, the flatter areas," said Nick. "Any more and I'd spend all my spare time working on the yard. Plus, some of the acreage is fairly steep."

He pointed to the pine-studded hillsides on either side of the property.

"I just mowed the lawn last night," said Nick, "The first time this year. We have such a short growing season in the

Hills. I won't plant my garden for a couple of weeks since there's still a chance we could get a freeze, especially since the creek flows through our property."

"Quite a bit cooler than Florida's climate," I added.

"More in line with England's," said Maurice.

"Except I wish we got as much moisture as England," I answered.

"Glad to meet a fellow duck," said Maurice. "Some people don't appreciate England's weather, but I quite enjoy the rain and cloudy skies."

"How often do you go back?" I asked.

"Three or four times a year, especially around the holidays. We keep a house over there."

"You're from England originally, aren't you?" I asked.

"I, and of course Robin, were actually born on the Isle of Man, off the coast of England, located squarely in the middle of the Irish Sea. When Robin and I were five, the family moved back to Manchester, England."

"Isn't the Manx cat also from the Isle of Man?" I asked.

"Why yes it is. The story goes that a few centuries ago, the original Manx swam to Ellan Vannin after surviving a ship wreck off the coast of the island."

"Ellen who?" I asked.

"Ellan Vannin," laughed Maurice. "The local name for the Isle of Man."

I smiled to myself when I realized how quickly we'd become comfortable with Maurice.

As we approached the back of the property, Gordon pointed to a small building and asked, "Is that what I think it is?"

"Yes indeed," said a grinning Nick. "An outhouse. It's where I do some of my best thinking. A place I call my own. I know Caroline doesn't use it because a roll of toilet paper in my commode lasts a couple of months. Let me give you fine gentlemen a tour."

Nick showed Maurice and Gordon the ins and outs of the outhouse. They were completely enthralled.

"Nice wood pile," Maurice said turning his attention to the neatly stacked rows of logs next to the outhouse.

"You just scored major brownie points," I said. "One of Nick's pride and joys is his wood pile."

We leisurely walked the perimeter of the lawn until we came to the creek. We tried out the simple foot bridge Nick and I had recently built over the spring. At Maurice's suggestion, the four of us sat on the bridge and dangled our feet over the edge. Shelby plopped down next to Maurice.

"I assume this spring flows to the nearby lake Gordon and I passed on our way here," said Maurice.

"Sheridan Lake, yep," I answered. "Do you like trivia?"

"I love trivia," replied Maurice.

"Sheridan Lake actually started out as a town, a county seat even. But, after it lost its status to faster growing Rapid City, the settlement turned into a ghost town. In the 1930s, a conservation group bought the land, constructed a dam, and turned it into a lake."

"A beautiful little lake, at that," said Maurice. "No doubt you make good use of it."

"Yes, it's my favorite fishing hole," said Nick. "And we take our canoe out on it every chance we get."

"This is so peaceful," said Maurice. "Do you have any neighbors?"

"Our closest one's a mile and a half back on the main road," I replied. "We love being secluded. We can't see the main road from the house and we usually don't hear road noise, except during the rally."

"What rally?" asked Maurice.

"The annual Sturgis motorcycle rally," said Nick. "It's held the first week in August."

"Sturgis is about an hour's drive from here," I added. "But during the rally, the bikers take over the entire Hills. It's exciting having them here. Every year we park our pickup where our driveway meets the main road, so we can watch the bikes go by. Sometimes bikers will stop and chat with us. We've met a lot of great people that way. Oh, and you should see the beautiful bikes."

"Do you ever go to Sturgis during the rally?" asked Gordon.

"We haven't in a couple of years," I answered. "But it sure is a sight to see. Main Street is lined with thousands of bikes, and bikers, in all sizes and shapes."

"I've gone to a couple of Daytona's Bike Weeks," said Gordon. "The bikers there tell me incredible stories about Sturgis."

"And there're probably all true," said Nick, "especially the campground stories. In my younger days, I witnessed things at the campgrounds I didn't even know could be done. I've been told that back in the seventies, it was even more risqué."

"It's fun when the bikers are here," I said. "But, I have to admit, it's nice to get back to relative peace and quiet once the rally's over."

Maurice leaned over to Gordon and the two of them whispered back and forth for a moment. I heard Maurice ask Gordon if he needed help. Gordon shook his head. "No, I got it."

Gordon stood up, brushed off his seat and said, "S'cuse me, Caroline and Nick, but I'll be back in a few minutes."

"Sorry about the secrecy," said Maurice, "but if you don't mind, I'd like to spend the night here. Gordo's going to retrieve my things from the B&B, although he'll still stay there."

We all waved to Gordon as he drove off.

"And who is this mild-mannered feline?" Maurice asked as an orange tabby rubbed against his back.

"That's Tom Cat, our mouser and bird watcher," I answered.

13

Maurice placed Tom Cat in his lap and gave him a scratch under his chin.

"When Tom started coming around here about five years ago," I said, "I put food out for him. He'd hang around for maybe a week at a time and then disappear. I think he had another family in the area and he was going between the two of us. One day I took Thomas to the vet to get him neutered and vaccinated. Since then, he sticks around here so I proudly claim him as ours."

"Tom Cat and I have something in common," said Maurice. "We share the same name."

"How's that?" I asked

"Gibb means tom cat."

"See," I responded. "You were destined to be here."

"And any moment now," said Nick, "all of us will be destined to move to the porch. The mosquitoes are starting their feeding frenzy."

"I'll meet you there," Maurice said as he took out a pack of cigarettes. "I need to have a smoke first."

Nick and I walked to the house while Shelby and Tom Cat stayed behind with Maurice.

Nick retrieved the pitcher of iced tea from the fridge as I went upstairs to see if Maurice's room and the guest bathroom were suitable for a VIP. They weren't, but I had a feeling Maurice wouldn't mind.

Although I imagined him to be friendly, I was surprised by how down-to-earth and trusting Maurice was. Damn him, who was he to have so much faith in us. Yes, I was beginning to experience a mini freak out. There was only one thing to do—devour half a dozen mini chocolates from the bag I had hidden in the guest closet, which I accomplished within a matter of seconds. To redeem myself I put one on Maurice's pillow.

By the time I got back downstairs, Maurice and Nick were sitting in the screened-in porch, sipping tea, and talking about the weather. Nick had found one of the few ashtrays we owned and had placed it on the patio table next to Maurice who was smoking another cigarette.

When I joined them Maurice said, "Since neither of you smoke, I'll confine my smoking to outside."

"We invited you to our house," I answered, "so you're welcome to smoke in the house."

To the best of my knowledge, no one had ever smoked in our house. However, I didn't want to put a crimp in his visit by insisting that he smoke outside. As I took the empty seat between Nick and Maurice, I made a mental note to find another ashtray to put in his room.

"So, Mo," I heard myself say. "I mean Maurice."

"No, please call me Mo. Most of my friends do. I fancy it myself."

"That reminds me, since you want to keep your visit low key, should we refer to you by another name when we're in public?" I asked.

"Incognito, I like that," said Maurice. "Got any suggestions?"

"How about your namesake, Tom?" I asked.

"Tom it is," Maurice said.

"So, what would you like to see tomorrow?" I asked. "Have you ever been to South Dakota before?"

"To tell you the truth, I had to do a little research to find out exactly where South Dakota's located. I knew it was near North Dakota, but that didn't help because I didn't exactly know where North Dakota was."

"By the way, what'd your research uncover about Nick and me?" I asked mischievously.

"Well, I started with an Internet search that didn't produce anything out of the ordinary," said Maurice.

"Or remotely interesting, I'll bet," I added.

"I can't begin to tell you the juicy stuff I uncovered," Maurice answered. "But seriously, I discovered you actually work as an events coordinator like you mentioned in your letter. And I found a research paper Nick wrote for the

15

forest service, something about soil conservation. Then I had Gordon do a more detailed background check. Again, nothing out of the ordinary. So, I sent Gordon on a reconnaissance mission of sorts."

"You mean he came to South Dakota?" I asked.

"A couple of weeks ago, actually," Maurice answered. "The only low mark in his report was the weather. It snowed the day he was here and apparently he hates snow."

"So that's why you didn't need directions to our house," I said.

"I remember the day it snowed," added Nick, "but I don't remember seeing Gordon or any unusual tracks in our driveway."

"No, you wouldn't have. He's that good. Gordon constantly surprises me with his ingenuity."

"I hope you understand why I needed to run the checks on you," Maurice continued, "which, I may add, were conducted above the law."

"Of course we understand," I said. "It is a bit unnerving though to realize how easy it is for someone to get personal information on you. I'm sure you've experienced that a few times in your life."

"I could tell you stories that would curdle your milk," said Maurice.

Someone knocked on the door. I sprinted indoors to open the front door for Gordon who had his hands full.

"Let me help you," Maurice said as he relieved Gordon of half of his load. "Caroline, which room do you want me in?"

"I'll show you," I said as I led Maurice and Gordon up the stairs.

"I'll put you in the Lincoln suite," I said as I led them to the room on the right.

"There's plenty of space here for your clothes," I said as I opened the closet.

Discreetly, I grabbed an ash tray from the closet's top shelf and hid it behind my back before placing it on the night stand.

"Oh, and sorry, but we don't get good cell phone reception here, so our land phone is your land phone," I said as I pointed to the telephone on the stand.

I led Maurice to the bathroom as Gordon went downstairs.

"I hope you don't mind, but we have well water. I think it tastes good, but some people make faces when they attempt to drink it. So if you're one of those civilized type, there's bottled water in the fridge here in the bathroom and in the kitchen. Have I forgotten anything?"

"There is one thing," answered Maurice. "Do you have an Internet connection? I brought my laptop and camcorder, so I could send pictures to my kids, Adam and Sam, while I'm here."

Pictures. I forgot to buy film for my camera. Mental note to buy a few dozen rolls of film tomorrow.

"My computer's set up in here," I replied as I led him to the other bedroom that also doubled as an office. I unhooked the phone line from my computer and left the cord on top of the desk.

"So you like to take pictures," I said. "Seems like you'd be sick of cameras since you probably have your picture taken all the time."

"I've always loved cameras," answered Maurice. "Even when I was young I'd make mini movies starring my family and neighborhood friends."

"Do you still have your old movies?" I asked.

"I do. I wouldn't give them up for the world."

When he said "world" I caught myself grinning.

"What'd I say?" asked Maurice.

"You said world. I love the way you say world. You soften the edges and make it sound so delicate especially compared to the way we Americans pronounce it."

"W-o-r-l-d," I said as I over enunciated, particularly the "r."

Then I tried to imitate his pronunciation, "Wuhld," I said and smiled again. "Well, I'll let you get settled in."

I walked down the stairs silently chiding myself for my strange behavior.

Chapter 3

WHEN MAURICE WALKED down the stairs a few minutes later, I noticed how striking he was. He wore all black—black boots, black jeans, a black long-sleeved t-shirt with the sleeves pushed up to three-quarter length, and a black baseball cap. His dark beard and moustache were neatly trimmed. His round, wire-rimmed glasses complimented his face. And he didn't appear to have an ounce of fat on his tanned frame. When he noticed I was looking his way, he showed off his beautiful white teeth by giving me an incredible smile.

"Mo, you light up a room with your smile," I said.

"Thank you. Smiling is such a simple act that can have such a dramatic affect," he answered as he joined Nick, Gordon, and me at the dining room table. "So, do you want to plan out tomorrow?"

"Is there anything in particular you two would like to see?" I asked.

"Gordon, what sounds good to you?" replied Maurice.

"Absolutely anything that does not involve snow," answered Gordon.

"That was the first thing on my list," Maurice said with a chuckle as he patted Gordon on the back. "Of course, we should visit Mount Rushmore and perhaps something having to do with Native Americans. Other than that I'm open for suggestions."

Nick spread out a forest service map of the Black Hills on the table. Within minutes, we decided our course of action for Saturday and talked about possibilities for Sunday.

Shelby, who had retrieved her brush from her basket of doggie paraphernalia, pushed her nose under my arm to remind me of her nightly brushing.

"No Shelby Lee, not tonight," I said.

"Look at those puppy dog eyes," said Maurice. "You can't refuse her. How about you comb her while I lark about on your piano. I get restless if I'm away from a keyboard any longer than a day."

"It's a deal."

Shelby and I situated ourselves on the rug in the living room while Maurice positioned himself between the piano and the bench. He looked my way as he placed his hands behind his back and flicked his palms upward to move imaginary tuxedo tails out of the way before he sat down. He briefly stretched his fingers before playing a few exercise bars. Then his music became more structured as he played a nice melody I wasn't familiar with.

"I've had this tune running through my head all day," Maurice said as he expanded the basic melody. After a few minutes he said, "I'll be right back."

He flew up the stairs to his bedroom and flew back down with a mini tape recorder in his right hand.

"I've got to get this tune down on tape," Maurice said before replaying his new song on the piano.

I finished brushing Shelby's left side and said, "Shelby, other side."

She immediately got up, turned a half circle, and lay on her other side.

"Nice trick," Maurice said as he looked over his shoulder.

I didn't even know he was paying attention to us.

"For now," he said speaking into the tape recorder, "I'll call this song 'The Other Side of Shelby.'"

Nick, who was jabbering with Gordon about the Sturgis rally, turned his head my way and gave me a wink.

"Nice little keyboard you have here," Maurice said.

He experimented with the piano's harpsichord, organ, and electric piano modes.

I took that as an opportunity to pull up a chair next to the piano bench.

"Mo, I have some blank sheet music if you'd rather write the music down," I said.

"Thanks Caroline, but it wouldn't do me a bit of good. I can't read music."

"Yeah right," I said.

"No, it's true. I can hardly read a note."

"You're pulling my leg," I laughed.

"I'm not—honest," Maurice said with both hands in the air as if he were being accosted.

"How do you remember it all?"

"There must be a compartment in my brain where I store the music. And, of course, tape recorders are a blessing."

"Do you like writing better by yourself or with your brothers?"

"I appreciate that I can write by myself. But, there's nothing better than composing with Barry or Robin, or better yet, with the both of them."

"Do you ever write with anyone else?" I asked.

"Interesting you should ask. I've also been composing with my kids, Adam and Samantha for a while now."

"How old are they?" I asked.

"Samantha is twenty-one and Adam is twenty-six."

"They add a whole new dimension to your music," I said

"Exactly," said Maurice. "It doesn't get any better."

"So, how many songs have you written or co-written?" I asked.

"Literally thousands. But, we've only recorded about seven hundred of them."

"Only!" exclaimed Nick.

"Since you have such an extensive catalog," I said, "and, you look so comfortable at my piano, will you take requests?"

"It's the least I can do. And you know me," Maurice added with a Groucho Marx impersonation, "I always try to do the least I can do."

"How about 'Smells Like Teen Spirit,'" I said.

Maurice began playing the opening bars of the Nirvana song.

"I was joking, Mo," I laughed. "But, I'm duly impressed. How about 'How Deep is your Love?'"

Shivers ran up and down my spine when his elegant fingers began playing "How Deep is your Love" on my piano, in my house. When he began singing, I thought I was in paradise.

"You can sing along, if you'd like," he said in between one of the phrasings.

"Ha, you're asking for trouble now," hollered Nick.

I shot Nick a mock dirty look. I don't have the best voice, but I have been known to hit a few consecutive notes correctly. So I sang the melody along with Maurice.

"That was great, Mo," I said as he played the song's final notes. "Now, how about 'Lonely Days.'"

Maurice played the song just like I'd heard it a hundred times before, beginning with the slow, haunting introduction. He even made my less-than-perfect melody line sound good thanks to his incredible harmony. We tightened it up a notch when we hit the rollicking, foot-stomping chorus.

"That was amazing, Mo," I said. "Now, how about something a little less mainstream, like 'Suddenly.'"

"You know that song?" asked Maurice. "Now I'm amazed."

"It's my favorite song off *Odessa*, particularly since you sing lead."

"I haven't played it in quite some time, but let's have a go."

After a brief warm-up, Maurice performed 'Suddenly' as if it were a part of his regular repertoire. He sang it in a low, playful voice. I added harmony to portions of the song, but for the most part, I let Maurice sing solo because I was having so much fun watching him perform.

"One more request," I said as he finished the song. "How about 'Trafalgar,' another one of my older favorites."

Maurice gave me a sideways smile before he began the accompaniment.

I got the feeling "Trafalgar" was one of his favorites because of the emotion he poured into the song. I added light harmony during the latter part of each verse and on the chorus, trying not to take away from his touching performance.

Nick and Gordon must have been as moved as I was because we all gave Maurice a hearty applause and a standing ovation when he finished.

"Thank you," said Maurice. "And to think 'Trafalgar' is just about a flock of birds."

"Say what?" I said.

"It's about a homeless man in London's Trafalgar Square who spends most of his day feeding the pigeons because he doesn't have anything better to do."

A light clicked on in my head.

"Mo, I need to show you something," I said. "This is unbelievable."

I rushed to my bedroom and came back with what appeared to be a rolled-up piece of newsprint.

"I bought this print last year after I saw a framed version of it in an art gallery in Nebraska, of all places. I immediately fell in love with the painting. Unfortunately, I couldn't afford the framed picture at the time, so I left the gallery empty handed. But I just couldn't get the image out of my mind. When I went back the next day to get one last look before I headed home, I learned the gallery had an unframed print that I could afford. I was planning on having it framed later this summer."

Keeping the print rolled up, I continued, "I thought the artist was nationally or even internationally known because the image is so striking. But, it turns out the painter, Richard DuBois, is from right here in the Black Hills."

I unrolled the newsprint to reveal a haunting dark blue and white watercolor of a man sitting on a park bench feeding pigeons.

"That's my Trafalgar," exclaimed Maurice as he jumped up from the piano bench. "That's precisely the image I had in mind when I wrote the song. You're right, Caroline, it is incredible."

"It's also yours," I said as I placed the print in his hands. "No doubt it was meant to be yours."

"I really shouldn't accept this, Caroline," Maurice said, "but I will. I love it. Thank you from the bottom of my heart."

"I need to tell you," he added, "that a part of me thought I was a fool for coming here this weekend. But, I've always thought you have to take chances once in a while. And I was right. Otherwise, I wouldn't have met the two of you. I'll remember your generosity every time I look at this picture."

Maurice noticed I was close to tears, so he put the picture down and gave me a heart-felt hug. Then Nick came up beside me, squeezed my right shoulder, and told me I did good.

After we gathered our senses, Gordon looked at his watch and said, "Well I think I'll call it a night. I'll see you all tomorrow morning."

"I'll walk you to the Land Rover, Gordo," said Maurice.

Chapter 4

I DIDN'T SLEEP well. The excitement from yesterday, coupled with my anxiety about today, prevented me from sleeping more than a couple of hours. However, being an early riser, I was still able to get out of bed when the alarm went off at five-thirty. Earlier in the month, Nick and I began jogging with Shelby on weekend mornings. This morning, Nick and Shelby went by themselves while I showered and got prepared in case Maurice was an early riser.

I put on a pot of coffee, turned on the TV long enough to check the news headlines, and then switched on the stereo.

"Good morning, Caroline," Maurice said as he came down the stairs a few minutes later.

"Good morning to you, Mo. How'd you sleep?"

"The bed was comfortable, but to be honest, not that well. The thrill of just being here kept me awake much of the night."

"Well, if it's any consolation, you look like you had a restful night. Nick and Shelby went jogging. They should be back soon."

"I was out on the balcony having a smoke when I saw them head out. Is that coffee I smell? If you'll show me where the cups are, I'll get myself fueled up."

I got a mug from the cupboard and poured his coffee myself.

Maurice took a sip and then flashed me a smile. "I can't believe what I'm hearing. Is that *Life in a Tin Can?*"

"Oh, I hadn't noticed," I replied with a grin. "I wanted you to wake up to a real South Dakota Morning."

I went to the CD and skipped back a few songs until I got to "South Dakota Morning."

"That song never sounded as good as it does right now," said Maurice.

"I know the album wasn't one of the Bee Gees best sellers."

"You're being kind, it was considered a disaster," added Maurice.

"Well I really enjoy it. I like the way the songs all flow together. Is there any particular story behind 'South Dakota Morning?'"

"Barry wrote it. I'm not sure what spurred him on, although he's always liked country-western music. If I can recall, South Dakota was in the news at the time, it must have been in 1972."

"You don't know how right you are," I said as I topped off his coffee. "In June of '72, a flood of the century hit Rapid City and the Hills."

"Were you here at the time?" asked Maurice.

"No, I was living on the other side of the state. But Nick lived in Rapid then. Fortunately, his family wasn't directly affected because their house was far enough from the flood waters. But a number of their friends and acquaintances died."

"How dreadful," said Maurice.

"Nick still gets emotional when the subject of the flood comes up. Apparently, a huge thunderstorm hit the area on the afternoon of June ninth. Most thunderstorms move on after an hour or so, but this one stayed right over the Hills, and in the process, dumped up to fifteen inches of rain."

"The deluge caused Rapid Creek, which begins in the high Hills, to spill over its banks," I continued. "When the creek's waters reached Rapid, it hit the city at full force. It roared into Canyon Lake, at the western edge of Rapid, and swelled the reservoir so much so that the dam gave way, causing a huge wall of water to gush through the city. A large residential area just down from the lake was the first to get pummeled."

Maurice listened intently as I continued.

"City officials had announced flood warnings. But many people were still caught off guard because the flooding had occurred so quickly. And there were power outages. And it was fairly late at night. When the dam broke it was ten-thirty, eleven."

"The flash flooding actually occurred throughout the Hills where, in some instances, there was little to no warning. Here in the central Hills, a number of people who were camped next to creeks were literally swept away by the swollen streams."

"How many people died in all?" asked Maurice.

"Two-hundred and thirty-eight. A week later, my parents and I came to Rapid and the Hills to pay our respects, of sorts. The destruction was unbelievable. Thousands of homes and businesses were damaged beyond repair. Most of the bridges over Rapid Creek were destroyed. And the mud—oh, it was everywhere. Even today, I can still recall the musty, rank odor of the mud."

After a pause Maurice said, "From what little I saw of Rapid City driving in from the airport, the town seems to have rebounded nicely."

"It really has. City officials condemned the land along Rapid Creek. They turned the flood plain into a beautiful park system with a popular bike path. And now better systems are in place to monitor potential emergency situations. Other cities that have experienced similar catastrophes have turned to Rapid as an example of how to rebuild after a tragedy."

"WE'RE BACK," ANNOUNCED Nick as he and Shelby entered through the main door.

Shelby rushed to Maurice to give him a morning greeting. Maurice rewarded her with a full-body massage. Shelby looked my way to see if I was envious of Maurice's attention toward her. When she realized her attempt to make me jealous actually made me smile, she cut her massage short and bounced over to me.

"Ha," said Maurice, "I know how I rate. Say, Nick, how's the weather this morning?"

"It's a bit chilly. We'll need to wear jackets today."

The phone rang as they continued their conversation about the weather.

"Hello," I answered.

"Good morning," said a vaguely familiar voice with a British accent. "Does Maurice happen to be there?"

"I uh, uhm, well, uhm," I hemmed and hawed, not knowing how I should answer.

I mouthed to Maurice, "It's for you!" and pointed to the phone.

"I'll take it," he mouthed back.

"Just a moment, please," I said in the receiver.

"Yes, this is the Nichols' residence," replied Maurice in a very respectable Midwestern accent. "How can I help you?"

After a brief pause, Maurice smiled and exclaimed, "Barry, you old dog, you found me."

Then he casually walked to the other side of the room. In the course of attempting to avoid getting caught eavesdropping, I was able to catch bits and pieces of their conversation.

"It seems cell phones don't work well here in the gulch. . . It's a long story, I'll tell you later. . . We were just headed out the door to Mount Rushmore. . . You want me to pick you up a souvenir or two?"

When their conversation appeared to include Nick and me, Maurice moved back toward us.

"Guess what we listened to this morning? . . Think about it. I'm in South Dakota, it's morning."

"You're right. How did you know? . . Like it was in a tin can," which Maurice followed with a hearty laugh.

"No, she doesn't want to talk to you. . . "Okay, I promise I'll call you later this weekend. . . I will."

Maurice handed the phone to me with mock disgust and said, "I told Barry you didn't want to talk to him, but he insists."

"Hello," I said in a voice much weaker than I would have liked.

"Hello Caroline, I'm sorry to have shaken you up earlier," said Barry. "I hope Mo isn't causing you too many problems. He's a hell raiser, that one."

I found my voice and replied, "We haven't gotten into too much trouble yet, but the whole weekend is ahead of us. By the way, 'South Dakota Morning' sounded wonderful."

"Maurice is just jealous he didn't write it," said Barry. "I wanted to thank you for inviting Mo to South Dakota. That way he's out of my hair for a few days."

A wild idea suddenly crossed my mind.

"Barry could you do a small favor for me. You can say no and I'll understand. But could you sing a few lines of 'Words' for me?"

"Anything for a friend of Mo's. Let me see if I remember the words. I think it goes something like this," he said before he started singing in his poignant voice.

"Smile, an everlasting…"

He stopped singing after the second verse and asked, "More?"

"Please, more."

Without missing a beat, he continued.

"Talk in everlasting…"

I mouthed the words all the way through.

"… your heart away."

"Barry, that was so beautiful," I said after he finished the final note. "Thank you so much."

"You're welcome. I'm glad you liked it. Well I hope you all have a wonderful time, and see to it that Mo stays out of trouble."

"I will, Barry," I replied, "And thanks again."

I hung up and turned to Maurice. "I hope I wasn't out of line, but I got Barry to sing 'Words' for me."

"I'm sure he enjoyed singing for you," said Maurice. "He's a good sport. But he thinks I'm a bit mad for coming here. I suspect though he's a bit green with envy. He's never been to South Dakota before."

Chapter 5

WE ATE A breakfast of cereal and fruit, which Maurice preferred over a larger meal. Gordon knocked on the door as I loaded the last of the dishes in the dishwasher.

"How was your night at the B&B, Gordo?" asked Maurice while Gordon helped finish off the pot of coffee.

"It went very well," Gordon answered along with a thumbs up.

"So, is everyone ready to hit the road?" I asked.

We grabbed our jackets and our touristy-type provisions. Gordon volunteered to chauffer us in the Range Rover. Nick and I agreed, sensing that Gordon knew the roads as well as we did. Maurice urged me to sit in the front passenger seat, but I insisted that he ride shotgun. He reluctantly agreed after I pointed out he would get better pictures of the Hills and Mount Rushmore from the front seat. He started filming as soon as we pulled out of the driveway.

A dozen minutes later we drove through the small town of Keystone.

"Do either of you remember Carrie Ingalls," I asked Maurice and Gordon, "one of Laura Ingalls Wilder's sisters from the Little House on the Prairie books?"

"I do," Gordon answered eagerly just before he turned beet red. "Apparently, that isn't something I usually reveal about myself."

"I would have pegged you as a Gunsmoke man myself," said Maurice.

"You're in good company, Gordon," I said. "I'm a Little House fan, too. Anyway, Carrie made a name for herself here in the Hills in the newspaper business and lived in Keystone for a while. Her relatives all thought Carrie would be the famous one in the family. But that was before her big sister, Laura, began writing books."

On the other side of Keystone, I pointed out Mount Rushmore in the distance. Maurice shot footage while Gordon maneuvered the Range Rover up the steep hill that led to the monument and the parking garage.

"Remember, we call Mo 'Tom' today," I said as we all hopped out of the vehicle.

"I'll even try talking with a South Dakota accent," Maurice said with a South Dakota accent.

We walked past the elevator in favor of the two flights of stairs.

"What are those?" Maurice exclaimed when we reached the top of the stairs.

"They're mountain goats," said Nick as Maurice filmed the small herd of horned and bearded creatures that donned long, white fur. "They love this area's steep, rocky terrain."

Maurice turned around, caught his first close view of Mount Rushmore, and said, "My God, will you look at that. It's magnificent."

He repeated "magnificent" a number of times and added "amazing" and "brilliant" as we walked past the pillars that displayed the flags of American States and territories. I offered to film Maurice in front of the faces.

"Better yet, I'll film the three of you," said Gordon.

Maurice handed his camcorder to Gordon and I gave Gordon one of the disposable cameras Nick had graciously bought for me minutes beforehand at the gift shop. Unbeknownst to Maurice, he was wearing rabbit ears in a couple of the pictures Gordon shot from my camera. I then took pictures of Maurice and Gordon in front of the presidents.

We walked down to the amphitheatre to get a closer view of the faces. A few people gave Maurice curious stares, which prompted me to call him "Tom." I didn't want to share him with other people, at least not so early in the weekend. Maurice alleviated my jealous streak by responding to my "Tom" calls with answers laced with a South Dakota accent.

"This is the best time of the day to view Mount Rushmore," I said. "The sculptor, Gutzon Borglum, said the morning sun highlights Mount Rushmore's features. And we're lucky it's a clear day. We usually get a lot of rain in May and since the faces are close to six-thousand feet in altitude, some unlucky tourists don't even get to see Mount Rushmore once they get here due to the fog."

"Caroline called the superintendent of Mount Rushmore yesterday," added Nick, "to make sure the faces would be visible for our visit today."

"Why thank you, Caroline," said Maurice. "Who are the presidents on the mountain? I know that's George Washington on the left and Abraham Lincoln on the right. But I'm not sure about the other two."

"Thomas Jefferson is next to Washington and Theodore Roosevelt is on Jefferson's other side," I said. "George Washington was selected because he was our first president and the commander of the Revolutionary army, apologizes to Britain."

"Apologies reluctantly accepted," Maurice said.

"Thomas Jefferson was the author of the Declaration of Independence and an advocate for westward expansion. He chartered the Lewis and Clark expedition, which happened to pass right through South Dakota. When Borglum was working on Jefferson, sightseers often mistook him for Martha Washington."

Maurice and Gordon laughed.

"Abraham Lincoln because under his leadership the slaves were freed and America remained one country. And Theodore Roosevelt because he promoted causes like conservationism and helped to establish the National Park system. And, you didn't hear this from me, but I've been told that without glasses, Theodore Roosevelt bears a striking resemblance to Gutzon Borglum, the sculptor."

"A humble man that Borglum," said Maurice. "Sounds a lot like me."

"Borglum had planned on carving the four from the waist up," I added. "But when he died in 1941, his son, Lincoln, was put in charge of finishing the monument. Lincoln made a few refinements, but because of this and that, what you see today is basically what the memorial looked like when Gutzon died."

"Were Gutzon and his son the only ones who worked on Mount Rushmore?" asked Gordon.

"Oh no. Borglum had a crew of five hundred or so men," I answered.

"What possessed Borglum to carve Mount Rushmore?" asked Maurice.

"In the 1920s, some state officials who wanted to draw more tourists to South Dakota came up with the idea of carving the likenesses of Wild West heroes in the needle-like granite formations close by. Somehow they managed to get Borglum, who had worked on Stone Mountain in Georgia, to come to the Hills to oversee the project. He liked the basic idea but thought a presidential theme would have more public appeal. He also scouted out a better location, this large granite mountain, which you see in front of you."

"Why's it called Mount Rushmore?" asked Gordon.

"Funny *you* should ask that, Gordon," I answered. "Even before Borglum came here, an attorney from New York, named Charles Rushmore, toured the Hills with acquaintances from the area, including Carrie Ingalls' future husband.

"What do you know," said Gordon.

"Rushmore would point to various peaks and ask their names," I continued. "When they came to this point, which didn't have an official white name, his companions joked, 'We'll call it Mount Rushmore.' And the name stuck."

"What do you mean official white name?" asked Maurice.

"Well, white settlers had a number of nicknames for the site," I said, "like Keystone Cliffs. What are some of the other names, Nick?"

"Sugarloaf Mountain. Cougar Mountain," answered Nick.

"And," I added, "it had been known to Native Americans as Six Grandfathers."

"How fascinating," said Maurice. "It never occurred to me there would be a Native American component to Mount Rushmore. The things I've already learned today."

Nick and I led Maurice and Gordon to the Presidential Trail to get the closest legal view of the faces.

"Does anyone ever climb the monument, like Cary Grant did in *North by Northwest*?" asked Maurice.

"Every once in a while," answered Nick. "But their euphoria is short lived because they soon find themselves in handcuffs."

"You like *North by Northwest*? I asked Maurice.

Maurice answered with an Alfred Hitchcock impersonation, "I absolutely love it."

"Do you remember the scene in the dining room at Mount Rushmore?" I asked.

"Where Cary Grant gets shot by Eva Marie Saint?"

"That's it. The next time you watch the movie, pay close attention to a boy who's sitting at a nearby table. You can see him plugging his ears just before the gun goes off. He was anticipating the loud noise because he'd experienced it in earlier cuts."

"Ha, you know I'll watch out for it," said Maurice. "So, can you tell me anything about that striking house toward the end of the movie? Is it a real house and is it around here?"

"I love that house, too," I answered. "Unfortunately, it doesn't exist."

"What a shame," said Maurice.

"You two must have visited Mount Rushmore hundreds of times," said Gordon. "Don't you ever get tired of it?"

"Never," answered Nick. "When we retire, I can see us coming here every week to have breakfast with the presidents."

I EASILY PERSUADED Maurice to accompany me to the ever-important gift shop. When we approached the Black Hills Gold jewelry display, I held up my left wrist to show him my Black Hills Gold watch. The tri-colored gold on the watch, like all Black Hills Gold jewelry, was hand-crafted in patterns of leaves, vines, and grape clusters and in shades of pink, green, and gold.

"I've seen this jewelry on the shopping network," Maurice said and then quickly added, "Not that I've ever watched that channel."

"Course not," I added.

"My wife and daughter and mother. . . for that matter, my son, would love these."

Maurice picked out necklaces, earrings, bracelets, watches, bolo ties, and money clips for his family and some of his friends. He even bought a ring for himself, which promptly found a home on his right hand.

"They're going to be so pleased," Maurice said as the cashier cheerfully rung up his order.

Next on our list were the t-shirt displays, where Maurice found half a dozen shirts to his liking.

"I almost forgot," said Maurice. "I need to pick up some extra special presents for Barry."

He selected a bright pink back scratcher and a plastic snow globe. "These should get a rise out of him."

When we exited the gift shop, Maurice noticed a piece of equipment on top of the building and waved in its direction.

"Is that a webcam?" he asked.

"It is."

"I'll have to remember to get on the monument's website when I get home so I can view Mount Rushmore any time I want."

We joined Gordon and Nick who were talking to a lanky, bearded fellow dressed like Abraham Lincoln. Apparently, they would rather talk to a president than browse in a gift shop. Go figure. At my request, the four of them posed like the faces on the memorial while I snapped a few pictures.

Before we returned to the Range Rover, Maurice put his left arm around me and gave me a half hug as he took another admiring look at the monument.

GORDON DROVE US around the back side of Mount Rushmore and stopped long enough for Maurice to shoot footage of Washington's profile.

Minutes later, we approached a small, picturesque lake. Nick navigated Gordon to the parking area so Maurice could film the scenery.

"This is a lovely lake not far from Mount Rushmore," narrated Maurice as the four of us walked toward the water. "What's the name of this lake?" Maurice asked as he panned the camcorder in my direction.

"Horse Thief Lake. It's a popular camping and fishing spot in the Hills. President Bush, number forty-one, even fished here during his presidency."

After a few more minutes of filming, Maurice made some sort of sign language to Gordon, who dutifully took Nick for a walk in the other direction.

I had a feeling Maurice wanted to talk to me about my spell of jealously back at Mount Rushmore. To make it easier for the both of us, I started the conversation.

"Mo, I need to apologize for the way I acted when I thought those people were going to approach you. I admit I was a bit jealous. But I had no right to prevent them from talking to you."

"I appreciate the way you were trying to protect me," said Maurice. "And, I know I said I wanted to keep my visit low key. But I truly enjoy signing autographs and having my picture taken with fans. Since only a handful of people appear to recognize me in the area, let's come up with a compromise."

I nodded my head as I thought about how diplomatically he was handling the situation.

"If someone asks me for an autograph, I'll sign it for them. But if you hear me using my South Dakota accent, that's your cue to call me Tom and come to my aid."

"It's a deal."

"Great. Now I thought I'd call Yvonne to see what sort of mischief she's gotten herself into this weekend."

Maurice produced a cell phone from him jacket.

"Tell her I say hello," I said.

Apparently, Horse Thief Lake has good cell phone reception because he connected quickly. Out of respect, I headed toward Gordon and Nick, but couldn't help but pick up Maurice's occasional laughter.

Nick was instructing Gordon on the intricacies of skipping stones across the water. Nick was a pro. He could make a stone skip up to seventeen times before it disappeared into the water. By the time Maurice joined us, Gordon could get five skips per stone, which was two better than my best.

"Caroline, Yvonne wants to talk to you," Maurice said. He handed the phone to me.

"Hi, Yvonne?" I said.

"Hello Caroline, it's so good to talk to you. Maurice seems to be having a splendid time. He went on about your home and the places you've taken him today. I do wish I could be there with you."

We chatted for a few more minutes before we said our goodbyes and I handed the phone back to Maurice.

After he ended the call I said, "She's great, Mo. Is she always that good-natured?"

"Except when she needs to knock some sense into me, which, luckily these days, isn't too often."

Chapter 6

CRAZY HORSE MEMORIAL is located within fifteen miles of Mount Rushmore on another large granite out-cropping. As we approached the sculpture from the road, Maurice and Gordon commented on the magnitude of the yet unfinished monument. Maurice began filming as we walked toward the visitors' center and museum.

He turned the camcorder toward me and asked, "So, what can you tell me about Crazy Horse, Caroline?"

"Well, did you know that the designer and sculptor be-hind Crazy Horse, Korczak Ziolkowski, worked on Mount Rushmore before he began Crazy Horse?"

"No I didn't," replied Maurice. "But I do now. What else should I know?"

"Well, Korczak, who was an award-winning sculptor, was approached by Native American leaders who wanted a monument to show that Indians also have great heroes. Crazy Horse was chosen because he was a highly revered Oglala Lakota warrior who died young but continued to in-spire his people even after his death. Because the location of Crazy Horse's burial plot has been kept secret, tribal leaders and Korczak envisioned this monument as an eter-nal tribute to him. I even heard Crazy Horse predicted he would come back to his people in stone."

"Fascinating," said Maurice. "Do go on."

"Well, Korczak began carving Crazy Horse in the late 1940s," I continued. "When Korczak's health began to fail, he drew detailed plans on how the carving should progress, so his wife and their ten children would be able to finish the

41

monument after he was gone. When Korczak died in the early 1980s, his family took over with no hesitation."

"How big is Crazy Horse compared to Mount Rushmore?" asked Gordon.

"Crazy Horse will be four times the size of Mount Rushmore when it's finished," I answered.

"And when will that be?" asked Maurice.

"The family doesn't have a target date. Or if they do, they're keeping it a secret. Like the leader Crazy Horse, they recognize that the journey is just as important as the final destination."

When Maurice turned off the camcorder, the four of us walked to the edge of the terrace.

"We're a ways from the mountain," said Maurice. "Any chance we can get a closer look?"

"For now, the only time you can get a better view is during the annual Volksmarch when you can actually walk on the outstretched arm and see the face close up. Speaking of which, the Volksmarch will be held in a couple of weeks."

"We've gone on a number of the Crazy Horse Volksmarches," said Nick. "It's great to see the progress. We always take pictures and compare them with previous years."

"Will you be going this year?" asked Maurice.

"Nah, maybe next year," I said. "This year I'm protesting their new 'no dog' policy. Shelby has always accompanied us and it wouldn't be the same without her, although, I have to admit, I may be one of the reasons behind the ban. One year when Shelby and I went alone because Nick had to work and I couldn't find anyone else willing to walk in the rain, Shelby dragged me off the path to do her business. I hadn't brought along a pooper-scooper bag because she'd gone at home. So I left her land mine where it lay. After it was too late, I realized I should have moved it further off the trail with a leaf or something, because the path was apt to widen when the number of Volksmarchers increased throughout the day, and I'll bet at least one unsuspecting hiker stepped in her surprise package. I feel bad whenever I think about it."

"But not bad enough to go back and pick up the poop," added Maurice.

"Apparently not," I replied with a grin and a glance at my watch. "Changing the subject completely, and I mean completely, it's lunch time. If you want to eat here, you two gentlemen can try a buffalo burger if you're so inclined."

"I'll try anything once," said Maurice.

We chose a table near the restaurant's front windows, so we could enjoy a panoramic view of Crazy Horse while we ate.

Just as we finished eating, two women in their 40s, a teen-aged girl, and a young boy approached the table.

"You're not one of the Bee Gees, are you?" asked one of the women.

"Why yes I am," answered Maurice with a smile.

"You're Mo," she said.

"Right again."

"I think I'm going to faint right here," she exclaimed. "I am one of your biggest fans. I have every single one of your albums. Could I have your autograph and take your picture?"

"Of course," answered Maurice.

"Their music was in *Saturday Night Fever*," said the second woman to the teenager.

The first woman handed a postcard of Crazy Horse to Maurice.

"What's your name, love?" asked Maurice.

"I'm Pauline, spelled just like it sounds."

"Your accent tells me you're not from here, Pauline," said Maurice as he began to write on her postcard.

Pauline giggled. "I'm not. I'm from New Jersey."

"What exit are ya?" asked Maurice.

Pauline giggled again. "Exit ten. You know New Jersey?"

"I have a few friends from there. What brings you to South Dakota?"

"My daughter, Nita, and I are visiting my friend, Jennifer, and her grandson, Peter, who are from Belle Fourche."

"And where is Belle Fourche, Jennifer?" asked Maurice.

Jennifer blushed and patted her left chest a few times. "Oh, now I'm going to faint. Uhm, Belle Fourche is at the edge of the northern Hills. This is Pauline and Nita's first trip to South Dakota."

"Mine, too," said Maurice.

"Are you having a good time?" asked Jennifer.

"I am having a fabulous time. Pauline, are you and Nita having a good time?"

"We're having a great time, especially now that we got to meet you."

"If you get to Belle Fourche, stop by and visit us," said Jennifer.

"Did you know," asked Peter, "that the geographic center of the United States is located near Belle Fourche?"

"No, I didn't, Peter," answered Maurice. "Thank you for sharing that interesting fact with me. Let's say the five of us go outside to continue our conversation and take some pictures. Excuse me, Caroline, Nick, I'll be right back."

"DOES HE EVER get tired of signing autographs?" I asked Gordon.

"Not to make him sound like a saint," answered Gordon, "because he'd be the first one to tell you he's not. But as long as I've known him, he's always appreciated his fans."

44

"He seems to go out of his way to make them feel comfortable," I said.

"You've got that right," added Gordon. "I'm constantly amazed by the way he interacts with people. You meet him and five minutes later you feel like you've known him for years."

"Is he always sincere, or does he ever put on an act?" asked Nick.

"With Moby, what you see is what you get."

Gordon motioned toward Maurice, who was surrounded by a couple dozen people. "It looks like a few more people have discovered him. I'd better get out there. Could you do me a favor and pay the bill?"

Gordon handed money to Nick and left before Nick could put up a polite offer to pick up the tab himself.

Chapter 7

THE SIGHTS AND sounds of Custer State Park were our next destination.

As we drove past the State Game Lodge, I said, "This was once called the summer White House because Calvin Coolidge spent a summer here during his presidency."

"And Dwight Eisenhower spent a few days at the lodge during his presidency, too," added Nick.

"I didn't know that," I said.

"I did," said Maurice.

"You did?" I replied.

"Of course. You knew that too, didn't you Gordo?" asked Maurice.

"Sure, I thought everyone knew that," said Gordon.

"You guys are incorrigible. Did you also know the Black Hills was considered as the site for the United Nations?"

"Now that I didn't know," said Maurice.

"Apparently, its somewhat remote location, compared to New York City, was a drawback."

"What a bunch of tenderfoots," said Maurice.

A pack of burros triggered a minor traffic jam ahead as people stopped to feed the burly animals. Gordon slowly inched the Range Rover toward the burros. I located three cereal bars from my backpack and handed them to Maurice, Gordon, and Nick. The trio shrieked like little boys when the burros took them up on their offer for free food. Maurice got out of the Range Rover so I could take a picture of him with his arms around his new buddy's neck.

After the burros snubbed us for people with fresh vegetables, we decided it was our cue to continue our travels on the Wildlife Loop with the prime objective of finding buffalo, which Maurice and Gordon had never seen before, except for on their plates at Crazy Horse. At the southern end of the park, we were lucky enough to spot a herd crossing the road ahead of us.

"They look like props out of a cowboy and Indian movie," said Maurice.

"Believe me, they're real," I said. "They look like docile, clumsy animals, but they can sure run fast. Seems like every summer an overconfident tourist gets a little too close to one. Then without warning the buffalo charges at lightning speed and, before the tourist can get out of the way, he gets gored by the buffalo's horns. I say he, because it's usually people of the male persuasion who think they can outrun a buffalo."

After a leisurely viewing of the buffalo from a safe distance, we drove to a prairie dog village and spent a few entertaining minutes watching the little creatures pop in and out of their holes in the ground.

Before Gordon started the Range Rover, Maurice volunteered to take over driving duties.

"Thanks, but I'm fine," said Gordon.

"I thought you might be tired," said Maurice. "Before we stopped to see the prairie dogs, I saw you stretching your fingers."

"Oh, you mean this," Gordon said as he straightened up the fingers on his right hand that had been grasping the steering wheel. "I was waving to the other drivers."

Gordon saw the perplexed look on Maurice's face, so he added, "They did it first."

"It's called the Midwestern wave," added Nick as Gordon pulled onto the road. "Sometimes the driver will only use one finger—the index finger," Nick quickly added.

"Normally older drivers, usually men, will initiate the

wave, and only to cars from their state or surrounding states. Here in the Hills, we normally acknowledge South Dakota, Nebraska, and Wyoming drivers. I assume they waved to Gordon since the Range Rover has South Dakota plates."

"Can I do it?" asked Maurice.

"Sorry, it's an informal rule that only the driver can wave," Nick answered. "Gordon, will you wave to this next car? It has Wyoming plates."

Gordon raised the index finger of his right hand from the steering wheel, but the other driver didn't reciprocate.

"The bugger, why didn't he wave?" asked Maurice.

"Could be Gordon caught him off guard, or he didn't notice," said Nick. "Or maybe he's not familiar with the ritual. My dad taught me the intricacies of the wave while I was in grade school. When I learned to drive at fourteen, I was so excited to finally be able to 'do the wave.'"

"IT'S CLOSE TO the top of the hour," Maurice said as he turned on the radio. "Do you mind if I catch up on the news, find out what's happening in the world?"

Scanning through the channels, he landed on a station that was playing the beginning guitar licks of a familiar tune.

"Keep it there," I yelled. "That's one of my favorite songs."

Maurice looked back at me and smiled. It took me a few seconds to realize that the song playing on the radio, "Jive Talkin'," was by the Bee Gees and that I was in the presence of a Bee Gee.

"Now this is what you call surreal," I said.

Gordon, who had spotted another herd of buffalo, pulled over to the side of the road. He and Nick got out of the vehicle to watch the buffalo while Maurice and I stayed put to sing along to the song. When the music began to fade, the two of us broke out in laughter.

"I know the story behind 'Jive Talkin',' it was your drive talkin'," I said as we got out of the vehicle. "But mind if I share my memories of the song?"

"I'd be hurt if you didn't," teased Maurice.

"I had a summer job as the clean-up girl at my aunt's beauty salon over on the other side of the state. The best part of the job was the Top 40 radio station we played at the shop. Whenever I'd hear the opening guitar riff of 'Jive Talkin',' my mood would instantly change from indifference to absolute joy. I remember getting the strangest looks from customers when I bebopped to the song."

"I wonder why," said Maurice.

"You should have seen their looks when I'd hear a commercial for *Jaws*," I added, which prompted Maurice to imitate the opening bars of the *Jaws* theme.

"Yes, even today when I hear that, I still think of 'Jive Talkin',' because they both came out the summer of '75. One of my favorite songs and one of my favorite movies."

"But wait, that's only part of the story," I continued. "Whenever I'd go to record stores after your *Main Course* album came out that year, I'd pick up a copy of the album, scan the front cover, and then longingly look at the back for a few minutes before I'd put it back on the rack."

"And why's that?" asked Maurice.

"You'll think this is bizarre, but it was because of the naked lady on the cover."

Maurice game me a strange look.

"Okay, it was only a drawing, and a small one at that, and it really didn't show anything. But I was a sixteen-year-old prude who didn't want to buy a record with nudity on the cover. I kept checking album covers hoping to find one with a fully clothed woman."

"I believe she was giving herself a milk bath," Maurice said, as he leaned on a guard rail and watched buffalo in the distance, "which is best done when you're not wearing clothes."

"Yes, I know," I said with a grin. "And you'll be happy to know that earlier this year I threw out my inhibitions and finally bought *Main Course*. And I kick myself for not buying it sooner. Normally, when I get a new CD, it takes me a few times through before I warm up to the unreleased cuts, if ever. But every single song on *Main Course* blew me away the first listen. It's an incredible album, in case you didn't know."

"Not to sound arrogant, but it is, isn't it," said Maurice. "Seventy-five was a momentous year for me. Yvonne and I got married in '75 after our *Main Course* tour. Earlier that year, we all went to Miami to work on the album, hoping the change of scenery would get our career back on track."

"Which it did," I interjected.

"Thankfully. We had hit rock bottom the year before. The only gigs we could get were at small clubs. Ironically, that valley in our career turned out to be the best thing that ever happened to me given that I met and fell head over heels for Yvonne while we were playing a club up in northern England."

"Isn't it funny how things work out," I said.

"I truly believe everything happens for a reason," said Maurice. "Like, if Lu and I hadn't of married and divorced, I would never have met Yvonne and we wouldn't have two wonderful children."

"You're talking about Lulu?" I asked.

"Sorry, yes. Lulu and I married in '69. We were so incredibly happy in the beginning. Unfortunately, our busy careers and this and that got in the way. We managed well for a couple of years or so, but then it got to be too much for the both of us."

Maurice lit a cigarette before continuing.

"It took me a while, but once I sorted out that my drinking played a role in the collapse of our marriage, Lu and I became friends again. That's the way it should be."

Maurice held out his left palm to catch a smattering of rain.

"If it's not too personal, Caroline, can I ask why you and Nick don't have children?"

Maurice caught me off guard. But since he was being so candid, I answered his question without hesitation.

"Well, when we began dating, we both said we wanted a couple of children. After we got married, we wanted time to ourselves before we started a family. Then we got comfortable being just the two of us. We're both very independent and the thought of having little beings that would require our constant attention scared us. But who knows. Nick and I are still relatively young and we like new adventures. So, I wouldn't be surprised if we had a child or two one of these years."

"If you do or if you don't, I know you and Nick will be just fine."

"Not to sound arrogant," I said, 'but I think so too."

When the smattering of rain turned to a downright pelting, the four of us sprinted toward the Range Rover and took our assigned seats.

"IS EVERYONE UP for the pigtails?" asked Nick when we approached the northeastern corner of Custer State Park.

"Pigtails?" answered Maurice.

"It's a windy stretch of Iron Mountain road not far from here," Nick said. "We can take another route if you suffer from car sickness."

"Let's give it a whirl," said Maurice.

Within a few minutes, Gordon guided the Range Rover down a road that spiraled one way and then back the other as it led us across a series of narrow, wooden bridges.

"This is wild," said Maurice. "I didn't know Disney World had rides in South Dakota. Must be part of Frontier Land."

I, however, was not enjoying the ride. Halfway through, my stomach started to give me warning signs.

"So how's everybody doing?" asked Nick.

When he spotted my ashen face, Nick instructed Gordon to turn off at a nearby scenic overlook. I quickly exited the vehicle and made it to a trash can before I gave my lunch a not-so-fond farewell.

Nick retrieved a rain coat from my backpack, ran outside, draped the rain coat around my shoulders, placed the hood over my head, and ran back to the Range Rover, all within a matter of seconds.

"Is she all right?" asked Maurice.

"She's fine," Nick said. "She's in denial, but she suffers from motion sickness."

"Shouldn't we go out there and help her?" asked Maurice.

"Nah, she's managing to throw up on her own just fine."

Maurice moved to the back seat.

After I felt confident my stomach wouldn't embarrass me further, I ran back to the Range Rover. I took my new position in the front passenger seat and motioned for Gordon to drive on.

"Sorry about that. I thought I was through with my car sickness days. I guess it's just like riding a bike. Once you learn how, you never forget," I said with a wry smile.

I popped a couple of aspirin in my mouth and followed them with a chaser of bottled water.

"If you don't mind me saying so, Caroline," said Maurice, "you don't look well. I assume taking you all to a nice restaurant for dinner doesn't sound too appealing."

I made a face at the mention of food.

By now, the rain was coming down in sheets.

"Well, I have some trout I caught earlier this month at Pactola Lake thawing in the fridge," Nick said. "How does it sound to everyone if I grill them for supper?"

"Sounds good to me," said Gordon.

"Ditto," said Maurice. "How about you Caroline?"

"I'll probably dine on soda crackers and water, so have at it."

WHEN WE GOT home, I excused myself to rest on the bed for a few minutes. Shelby, ever the comforter, lay down on the floor next to me.

Chapter 8

"SUPPER'S READY," NICK said as he nudged me from my nap. "You've been asleep for almost an hour. Come to the table. Maybe you'll feel like eating."

"Something smells good," I said. My stomach let out a growl.

The table was set with grilled trout, oven-baked biscuits, and a spinach salad.

"Mo and Gordon helped," Nick said when he noticed me admiring the table.

Within a matter of minutes, we devoured most of the food before us, except for the big plate of soda crackers that someone had placed next to my plate.

"That was excellent," Gordon said, rubbing his stomach. "I hate to eat and run though, but I've got to take care of a few things tonight."

Maurice went outside with Gordon and the two talked on the porch for a few minutes before Maurice came back in and began clearing the table.

"You don't need to do that," I said.

"But I do," replied Maurice. "I like to make myself useful."

Nick started a fire in the fireplace and turned on the TV while Maurice brought me dishes.

When the table was cleared, Maurice said, "If you don't mind, I'll be a few minutes upstairs. I want to send a stream of video to my kids."

I combed Shelby while Nick read the paper and watched the weather channel.

"Things are fine on the home front," announced Maurice as he cavorted down the stairs. "They can't wait to see more of the Hills when I get home. So what do you two normally do on a Saturday night?"

"We used to don our disco clothes and go dancing," I said. "But those wild days are behind us. Actually our evenings are pretty boring. Nick and I usually play hard during the day and recuperate once we get home. How 'bout you? What do you do on Saturday nights?"

"We might go out to dinner, or invite friends or family to our home, or go over to one of their houses. We're often content to just stay at home and watch movies. I demystify the exciting life of a celebrity."

"Didn't you party with the 'in crowd' when you got started in the business?" I asked.

"John Lennon was probably one of the first people I partied with," answered Maurice.

"You're kidding," Nick said.

"I assume you've met all the Beatles," I said.

"They were all great guys. In fact, they were some of the first to encourage us when we were making it big in England. I got to know John and Ringo the best. Ringo and I were even neighbors for a while and hung out together almost every night."

"That sounds like trouble with a capital T," I said.

"More than once that was the case, yes," answered Maurice.

"Were you influenced musically by the Beatles?" asked Nick.

"Of course, like everyone else," replied Maurice. "I was just picking up the bass guitar when the Beatles exploded onto the scene. Paul was, and still is actually, such an incredible bass player that he became my informal bass instructor. I'd teach myself to play the bass line on every Beatles' song just like Paul did. Barry and Robin and I were all wild about their music. When the Beatles came to Australia in '64. . ."

"The same year they came to the States," I interrupted.

"Yes, quite a significant year for them. When they came to Australia where we were living at the time, we knew we were headed in the right direction because we'd been writing and recording similar music even though we were only in our mid-teens."

"So it really is fitting that the Bee Gees starred in the *Sergeant Pepper* movie," I said.

Maurice made a comical frown.

"I know the critics panned the film," I added. "But I thought it was entertaining and the soundtrack was great. I saw the movie when it first came out in the late seventies."

"You and a dozen other people," laughed Maurice. "*Sergeant Pepper* was one of our few commercial failures. When we were first approached with the idea of making *Sergeant Pepper*, we had mixed feelings. Turning such a monumental album into a movie would be sacrilegious. But we were such enormous Beatles fans that, after the first wave of apprehension, we literally jumped at the chance."

Maurice made a wry smile.

"As it turned out, we should have looked before we leapt. Halfway through filming we realized it was going to bomb. We're not ones to quit when the going gets tough, mind you. But in this case, we begged and pleaded to get out of the movie."

"Well, if it's any consolation," I said, "you looked like you were having fun."

"You're right about that. We had a fabulous time making the film. I truly enjoyed working with Peter Frampton and George Burns, the whole lot really. My greatest thrill though, was working with George Martin, who was brought in as the movie's musical director."

"The Beatles' producer?" I asked.

"The one and only," replied Maurice. "The man's a genius. Working with him was quite a dream come true."

"Since we're on the subject of movies," added Maurice, "I wouldn't mind spending the night watching a good one."

"Well you're in luck," said Nick. "We have a stockpile of movies on VHS and a few on DVD. Take your pick."

I went to the kitchen to make popcorn while Nick and Maurice scanned through the movies.

"This is one of my favorites," announced Maurice as he held up *Young Frankenstein*. "Do you mind? I haven't seen it in years."

"That's one of our favorites, too," I said.

Nick and I spent the next couple hours watching *Young Frankenstein* with Maurice Gibb. Life can't get much better.

WHEN THE MOVIE ended, Maurice said his good nights and started up the stairs. Shelby trailed behind him.

"Shelby Lee, where do you think you're going?" I asked.

She looked back at me with her puppy-dog eyes.

"If it's okay with you," said Maurice, "I wouldn't mind her sleeping on the floor in my room. She'd be good company."

"Go ahead," I answered. "But feel free to send her downstairs if she bothers you at all."

Chapter 9

A FEW MINUTES after I got the coffee started, Maurice and Shelby greeted me, one with a "Good morning Caroline," and the other with a wiggle butt.

"Well good morning, Mo," I answered as I scratched Shelby behind her left ear. "How'd you sleep?"

"I fell asleep the moment my head hit the pillow and I didn't stir until Shelby nudged me awake a few minutes ago. I assume she needs to go out."

"The coffee's almost ready. Help yourself while I let Shelby out. C'mon Shell Bell."

"If you don't mind I'll take her out," said Maurice.

"You sure?" I replied.

"There's something in it for me—I want to try out the outhouse," Maurice said.

He grabbed his jacket and they both went out the front door to do their morning business.

"I could have stayed outside all morning," Maurice said when they returned a few minutes later. "Yesterday's rain left everything unbelievably stunning."

Maurice placed the Sunday paper on a bar stool by the kitchen counter.

"I love the morning after a rain, too," I said. "Hey, thanks for getting the paper, Mo."

"It was actually Shelby's idea. She invited me to walk with her to get the paper."

"Good girl, Shelby," I said as I gave her a full head massage. "And to think Mo thought he had a choice in going with you."

Shelby showed her appreciation by thumping her tail loudly against the wall.

"She's my little drummer girl," I said. "She loves to express herself with her tail."

"And she keeps pretty good time, too," Maurice said as he headed up the stairs. "I'm off to shower. See you in a few."

Nick appeared a few minutes later in a remarkably good mood for not being a morning person, due in part to the extra hour of sleep he got since he didn't go jogging with Shelby.

Maurice looked refreshed and vibrant when he came down the stairs for the second time.

"Morning Nick. Morning again, Caroline."

Nick and I glanced at each other and smiled because Maurice wasn't wearing his cap. He caught sight of our body language.

"Hope you don't mind the au natural look this morning. Sometimes it feels good to go without a hat."

"You're very handsome either way," I said honestly. I was thrilled Maurice felt comfortable in our presence.

I made omelets for breakfast. We needed extra energy to carry us through the active day we had planned.

After the hearty breakfast, we sipped our coffee in the screened-in, heated porch and watched the deer nibble at the grass. Shelby assumed her new position next to Maurice.

"Do you get a lot of wildlife in your garden?" asked Maurice.

"Besides deer," answered Nick, "we get turkey, rabbits, squirrels, chipmunks, an occasional bobcat and coyote. And look who's here—the bighorn sheep."

Nick pointed toward half a dozen rugged-looking animals with short brownish-gray fur and curled-back horns.

"They make a stop in our yard almost every day," said Nick.

"The wildlife is a mixed blessing," I added. "We love sharing habitat with the animals, especially since they were here first. But it's frustrating when you plant flowers and shrubs and the animals think you've planted the foliage for their palate. The deer even snack on roses. The thorns don't deter them in the least."

"Are there bears in the Hills?" asked Maurice.

"Funny you should ask," answered Nick. "There have been a few unsubstantiated sightings."

"I didn't know that," I exclaimed. "Why didn't you tell me?"

"Probably because I knew you didn't want to hear it," answered Nick. "Like when you learned about the mountain lions in the area."

"Have you ever seen a mountain lion?" asked Maurice.

"No, and I don't want to," I answered.

"Well, I wouldn't mind seeing one," replied Nick, "But at a comfortable distance."

Someone, I assumed Gordon, knocked on the front door.

"Come in," I said.

I sprinted toward the front door.

Gordon accepted a cup of coffee before we joined the others on the porch.

Tom Cat swaggered through the cat access on the porch door and then dropped a green, six-inch snake at Maurice's feet.

"Looks like you've made a friend," Nick said as he quickly picked up the live snake. He then opened the porch door and set the snake down in the grass.

"He was giving you a present," Nick said as returned to his chair.

"Thank you, Thomas," said Maurice, "but I've already had my breakfast, chum."

Maurice reached down to scratch Tom behind his ears. "I assume that wasn't a venomous snake."

"No, it was just a garter," answered Nick. "However, one of the most dangerous creatures in the Hills is another type of snake—the rattlesnake. A rattler's bite can be fatal if you don't get treatment. Fortunately, you rarely come across one and if you do, it'll probably warn you by shaking the rattles on its tails. The best thing to do then is to back away slowly and remember that it's just as afraid of you as you are of it."

"If you get bit," asked Gordon, "how long do you have before you need to worry?"

"Well, anywhere from twenty minutes to a couple of hours," answered Nick. "But I can't remember anyone dying from a rattlesnake bite in the hills. I'm not saying it's not possible, but it's very rare. However, we still like to take precautions, like carry walking sticks and check before we sit down in rocky areas. And we usually take Shelby with us when we go for walks. She's forewarned us at least once."

"By the way," I asked, "do either of you mind if we bring Shelby with us today?"

"We'd love to have her," responded Gordon. He was apparently beginning to appreciate the many advantages of a good dog.

"I need to warn you all that I used to be a Rattlesnake," said Maurice. "That's the name Barry and Robin and I used the first time we ever performed in public."

"Did people have to carry walking sticks around you?" asked Gordon.

"Hardly, we were quite harmless. Robin and I were seven or eight at the time. I remember it was right after Christmas. We had planned on miming to a record at a cinema near our home in Manchester, England. The manager would let kids perform between films. As luck would have it, on the way to the cinema that day, I dropped the record we were going to use, and it broke into a million bloody pieces. Since we didn't have time to glue them all back together, we decided to go on stage anyway and sing the song ourselves. As I recall, the kids loved us because we stayed up for a couple more songs. The manager even paid us."

"So, you turned professional at the ripe age of seven?" I asked.

"No, we were hardly polished enough to be considered professionals."

"Is that the first time the three of had ever sung together?" asked Nick.

"Oh no, we started singing together probably when Robin and I were six and Barry was nine. We'd sing together at home, first in the bedroom and then onto various other rooms. If I can recall, the acoustics in the bathroom were the best. Barry picked up the guitar around that time. He used to play this crude homemade guitar before my parents finally gave into his pleas to buy him a real one. Anyway, with Barry on guitar, the three of us started singing the popular tunes of the day. When Barry started composing not long after, we'd add his songs to our repertoire."

"I assume you sang in unison back then," I said.

"In the very beginning, but it didn't take long before we were harmonizing. It came so natural to us that we didn't think anything of it. We thought everyone could sing like us."

"When did you realize you had something special going on?" I asked.

"Probably when relatives would mistake us for the radio. My dad was a musician at the time. A bandleader and a drummer. When he realized we had talent, he taught us all sorts of techniques, like how to tighten our harmony, like the Mills Brothers and the Everly Brothers. Not long after, Barry and Robin and I decided we wanted to sing for a living and we made a pact that nothing would get in our way."

"I can't imagine having such focus at such an early age," I said. "When I was six I didn't have the slightest idea what I wanted to do when I grew up. I still don't. That's quite amazing, Mo."

"Not really," said Maurice with a smile. "We weren't good at anything else, so it was natural to continue with the one thing we knew how to do. We weren't particularly good students and we were a handful to control. I cringe when I think back at all the problems we caused our parents. I nicked a couple of things from around the neighborhood and Barry and Robin were two-bit arsonists. Their little pyrotechnic displays actually got the family kicked out of England. The local constable urged my mum and dad to move the family to Australia to avoid pressing charges."

"No," I said incredulously.

"It's true," said Maurice.

"Did your parents want to go?" asked Nick.

"Not particularly. But they had an adventurous streak in them, so they weren't too upset at being pushed onto another continent. Plus, all of us kids were eager to go, including Lesley, my sister. She's a year-and-a-half older than Barry."

"Did she ever sing with you?" I asked.

"Occasionally, yes. Lesley has a beautiful voice. But, she used to be afraid to sing in public."

"Was Andy born yet?" I asked.

"He was, uh, let me see."

Maurice calculated in his head.

"Andy was five months old when we boarded the ship for Australia."

"I bet that was an adventure in itself," said Nick.

"We had a smashing good time. Besides traveling by liner for the first time and visiting exotic places like Egypt, Barry and Robin and I spent most of the trip entertaining the other passengers."

"As paid performers?" asked Nick.

"Oh no. We gave impromptu performances. We'd start singing on the deck and before long, a group of people would gather around and ask us to sing their favorites. I remember my parents looking on in disbelief."

"We became the darlings of the ship," continued Maurice, "But by the time we finally reached Australia a month later, I, for one, was relieved to be on dry land."

"Where'd you live in Australia?" I asked.

"Initially, in Queensland, in the northeast."

"Did you like Australia?" asked Nick.

"I loved it, for the most part. The whole family did. My parents were thankful Australia seemed to keep the three of us urchins out of trouble. By then, music was consuming most of our free time. My dad, who was our manager at the time, started us out at local fairs. Then we moved on to clubs."

"You don't mean night clubs, do you?" I asked.

"Night clubs would be too kind of a description," answered Maurice. "They were actually bars, most of them pretty rugged. Now there was a learning experience you wouldn't get in any classroom."

"You were still in school at the time, weren't you?" I asked.

"I don't think Barry was. Robin and I were. But we dropped out soon afterward. We were all of thirteen when we left school."

"I didn't know that," said Gordon.

"That explains a lot, doesn't it Gordo," said Maurice. "Anyway, the start of our big break came the day local disc jockey, Bill Gates, heard us sing between runs at a race track."

"I imagine that's a different Bill Gates than the one who owns Microsoft," said Nick.

"Our Bill Gates had a radio show that he'd feature us on regularly. He also helped us settle on our name. There were so many B.G.'s floating about—Brothers Gibb, Barry Gibb, our mother Barbara Gibb, Bill Gates—that by consensus we decided on the Bee Gees."

"The Bee Gees," I repeated. "It's short, and catchy, and easy to remember."

"I assume your radio exposure increased your popularity," said Nick.

"That and our television show," said Maurice.

"You had your own TV show?" I said. "How old were you then?"

"That was 1964. I would have been thirteen, fourteen. We didn't just sing on the show. We threw a lot of humor into our act. We were quite the comedians."

"Like the Three Stooges," I said.

"Yes, and I was Curly, nyuck, nyuck. Our primary audience at the time wasn't even teenagers. It was their parents. They loved the physical comedy bits we threw in our act. If we hadn't made it as musicians, we probably would have become comedians."

"I can see that," said Gordon.

"Apparently music was our true calling though," continued Maurice, "since later that year we finally managed to get a song in Australia's top twenty. It was called, 'Wine and Women,' one of Barry's compositions. By then we were just singing Barry's songs. Even early on, he was quite a prolific songwriter."

"He sounds pretty mature to be writing about wine and women at . . . how old would he have been?" I asked.

"Probably sixteen. I don't know how he came up with such mature themes for his songs at that age. But the way we got into the top twenty was quite adolescent, although we'd do it again in a heartbeat. We had a fan base. . ."

"Even back then?" asked Nick.

"We had a small, but loyal following by then," answered Maurice. "We gave each member of our fan club money with instructions to buy copies of 'Wine and Women.' And it worked. We made the charts."

"Was that the first song you ever recorded?" I asked.

"No, that would have been a Barry composition called 'The Battle of the Blue and the Grey.' It got some respectable airtime in Sydney. But the B side, another Barry composition called 'The Three Kisses of Love' turned out to be more popular."

"Can you sing a few bars for me?" I asked.

"You're asking for trouble so early in the morning," said Maurice, "but here goes."

"Kiss me once. . ."

Maurice proceeded to sing the first verse.

"I'm impressed, I said. "What a pretty song."

"Yes, it is, but enough about me already, don't you think," said Maurice.

"For now, maybe," I said, "but not for long."

Maurice got up from his chair and stretched his arms. "What mountain are we climbing today?"

"Harney Peak," I answered as we all went in the house. "But we won't actually be climbing, more like hiking. Nick and I packed supplies and snacks in the backpack. And here are water bottles to hook on our belt loops."

"Not to spoil the party," said Gordon, "but it's chilly outside. Don't you think it's too cold to hike?"

Nick looked at the outdoor thermometer. "It is just 47 out. But, by the time we get to the trailhead, it'll warm up some. And once we get moving, we'll probably take our jackets off."

WE ALL AGREED I should sit in the Range Rover's front passenger seat since the road to the trailhead included a number of switchbacks. Shelby, who's not prone to bouts of motion sickness, happily took her place in the far back.

Ten minutes later we arrived in Hill City.

"Hill City is known as the Heart of the Hills," I said.

"What a charming town," said Maurice.

"It is now," I said, "But when Hill City was first established, it was far from charming. Old-timers say early Hill City consisted of a church on either end and a mile of hell in between."

"Sounds like my kind of place," said Maurice. "Was Hill City a gold town?"

"Almost, but no," I answered. "Miners from Custer, about fifteen miles south of here, moved to this area in search of gold, but they found tin instead, so you should feel right at home here, Mo."

"Because of *Life in a Tin Can?*" asked Maurice

"That and Tin Tin," I added.

"You know about Tin Tin?" asked Maurice.

"What's Tin Tin?" asked Gordon

"Many years ago, I produced for a group called Tin Tin," said Maurice.

"Toast and marmalade . . . ," I sang.

"I'm impressed Caroline," said Maurice.

"With my singing or my knowledge of Tin Tin?" I asked.

"Both?" answered Maurice. "So, what's this about the city of Custer? I assume it's named after General Custer."

"You know about Custer?" I answered.

"Of course," replied Maurice. "I love history, particularly when it comes to the Old West. What brought Custer to the Black Hills?"

"Well, because pioneers from the east were moving westward," I answered, "Indians were forced to relocate farther west, which they didn't particularly appreciate."

"Imagine that," said Maurice.

"In an attempt to appease the Native Americans," I continued, "the government signed a treaty with a number of the Sioux Tribes in the region. The Fort Laramie Treaty of 1868 promised the Indians ownership of land in the upper plains area, including the Black Hills, for the establishment of a great Sioux Nation reservation. The Black Hills were particularly significant to the Indians because they always considered, and still consider, the Hills to be sacred."

"In 1874," I continued, "an expedition led by Custer came to the Hills to map out the area and to control the bands of Indians that didn't sign the treaty. Those were the official purposes of the expedition. But as it so happened, a few geologists came along for the ride. So, unofficially, Custer and his men came to the Hills to confirm rumors of gold in the area. It didn't take the party long to locate gold near what is now the town of Custer. News traveled quickly, even back then, and within a matter of months, the population of Custer grew to over five-thousand people. So many people came to the Hills so quickly that it was nearly impossible to keep them out."

"So much for the Fort Laramie Treaty," said Maurice.

"Two years later, even larger amounts of gold were discovered in the Lead-Deadwood area, north of here," I added. "By that time, the government had given up trying to keep people out of the Hills."

"Didn't the Indians ultimately do Custer in?" asked Maurice.

"You know your history," I replied. "A couple of years after his expedition to the Hills, Custer and virtually all the Seventh Cavalry soldiers in his immediate command were killed about 400 miles north of here. Many Native Americans call it the Battle of the Greasy Grass, although most people around here know it as the Battle of the Little Bighorn, while others know it . . ."

"As Custer's Last Stand," completed Maurice.

Chapter 10

SYLVAN LAKE, LOCATED at the base of Harney Peak, is a relatively small, man-made lake with moss-covered boulders rising out of the water in seemingly strategically-placed positions.

When we arrived, the sun glistening off the water produced diamond-like sparkles across the lake.

"Yet another beautiful lake," said Maurice. He got out his camcorder and shot some footage.

"If you think this is stunning," I said, "wait 'til we get to the top of Harney."

I made a pit stop at the bathroom near the trailhead since there weren't any facilities for people of the female persuasion on the trail. Men, on the other hand, had plenty of trees at their disposal.

Shelby loved to hike Harney and I took advantage of her energy. I turned her leather leash into a makeshift umbilical cord by placing the end with the clasp through the other end's loop handle. I then stepped through the circle, tightened it around my waist, and hooked the clasp to Shelby's collar.

"That's cheating," Maurice said when he noticed Shelby pulling me along the path.

"How long of a hike is this?" asked Gordon

"The trail we'll take," Nick answered, "trail number nine. . ."

"Number nine, number nine," Maurice and I chanted in unison before we burst out in laughter.

"What's so funny?" asked Nick.

"You know, number nine, number nine," I answered. "From the Beatles *White Album*."

"Anyway," Nick continued, "trail number nine is six miles round trip. Most people make it in four to five hours. Our best time is just over two."

Nick noticed a concerned look on Gordon's face.

"But don't worry," Nick added. "We don't need to set any records today. We'll put Shelby on cruise control."

The gentle slope of the first five minutes of the trail gave a false impression to hikers who thought Harney would be a walk in the park. Soon enough the path steepened.

"We like to climb Harney at least once a year with people who haven't hiked it before," I said to Maurice and Gordon.

"We're honored," said Maurice.

"I hope you feel the same way when we're finished," I answered.

Shelby was in the lead pulling me along as planned. She wanted to go at a faster pace, but I kept her at a slow trot. I didn't want her to tire us out in the first fifteen minutes. Maurice was walking next to me on the seven-foot wide path and Gordon and Nick were a few paces behind.

"Harney Peak's the highest point in South Dakota," I said, "at just over seven-thousand feet. It's the highest peak between the Rockies and the Pyrenees in Europe, north of the Tropic of Cancer. Can't forget the Tropic of Cancer."

Shelby let out a whine when she spotted a squirrel. Although dogs on the trail are supposed to be leashed, I let her chase after the squirrel to run off some of her energy.

"I'm so glad you took us up on our offer," I said to Maurice. "To tell you the truth, when I wrote my letter I didn't expect a response. But from the minute I decided to write it, I'd thought about what it'd be like if you did end up visiting us."

"Have I met your expectations?" asked Maurice.

"And then some. You actually turned out to be much more down to earth than I imagined. But at the same time, you have this . . . magic about you. It's hard to describe."

"Do you send many fan letters?" asked Maurice.

I sensed he rerouted the subject because I had made him self-conscious.

"The note I sent you was the first fan letter I'd ever written."

"Well, I'm flattered," Maurice said in a serious tone. "What prompted the letter?"

"It actually started out because of my motion sickness, which you can attest to first hand. I fly quite a bit for work and since reading on planes makes me woozy, I have plenty of time to daydream. A couple of months ago, when I was flying back from D.C., I thought about who I'd invite on a tour of the Black Hills if the sky was the limit. My first list consisted of historical people like Queen Elizabeth I and Jesus and Abraham Lincoln. Others that made the list were Edgar Allen Poe, Gandhi, Shakespeare, Benjamin Franklin, Cleopatra."

"Benjamin Franklin and Cleopatra together," said Maurice. "Now that's something I'd like to see."

"Thank you. Who else did I invite?" I continued. "Vincent van Gogh, Mozart, Elvis, Judy Garland, Lucille Ball, John Lennon, George Harrison. Then I limited the list to my contemporaries, minus family and friends, and came up with people like Nelson Mandela, Paul McCartney, Ringo Starr, Stephen King, Julia Child, Steve Martin, Ellen DeGeneres, Dick Francis. . . ,"

"The British mystery writer?" asked Maurice.

"Yes, isn't he great? Another of my favorite writers is Bill Bryson who could chronicle the entire event. I also included Buzz Aldrin. . . ,"

"Buzz Aldrin," repeated Maurice. "The name's familiar, but I can't quite place him."

"He's the second man to set foot on the moon. I think he'd be such an interesting guest."

"You put a lot of thought into this, didn't you," said Maurice.

"I really did. I have the complete list at home if you ever want to look at it, which of course also includes the Bee Gees."

"Sounds like quite the get-together," said Maurice. "It would have been fun listening in on Ellen DeGeneres and Julia Child's conversation."

"That's what I thought. But of course, my fantasy tour was just that—a fantasy. I think it's a shame though that you live in the same moment in time as people you deeply admire, but you don't get a chance to thank most of them."

"I assume you know," said Maurice, "that many remarkable people in the world aren't well known."

"Oh, I couldn't agree more," I said. "Some of those who made my list are interesting people I've personally met throughout the years. One is a retired janitor who lived the life of a hobo during the Depression by hitching rides on freight trains all across the country. He has enough stories to fill a library."

"So, to answer your question," I continued, "why did I invite you? Because my dream tour party wasn't possible, I asked myself, 'What is possible?' If I could invite just one person to the Hills, who would I invite? I decided it had to be someone I admire, someone who's led an interesting life, who has a great sense of humor, who shares some of the same interests as me, who's still at the top of their game, someone I felt I could connect with easily. You came out as number one on my list."

"Even though you just recently rediscovered the Bee Gees?" asked Maurice.

"Probably because I just rediscovered the Bee Gees. When I played your latest CD, I realized your creative juices are just as strong, if not stronger, than they've ever been.

That's quite an accomplishment. You still have that drive. And I remembered enough about you and the Bee Gees from the sixties and the seventies to know you've led quite an interesting life."

"Why choose me rather than Robin or Barry?" asked Maurice.

"You've always been my favorite," I replied. "I'm impressed with the number of instruments you play and with your kinetic personality. Plus, you're so good looking."

I meant the last comment to be lighthearted, but I felt my face blush afterwards. Maurice must have noticed because he gave me a friendly hug.

"Now it's your turn to confess, Mo," I said. "Why did you decide to visit us? I'm not a member of your fan club, and from my letter you know I wasn't faithful during the disco era."

"Let me begin by saying that I owe the members of my fan clubs more than they'll ever know," said Maurice, "hundreds of whom I've have the pleasure of meeting. I appreciate their loyalty, especially through the hard times. That said, why did I accept your offer rather than visiting one of them? Things literally fell into place, almost like this weekend was destined to happen. For one thing, you don't seem to know everything there is to know about me, and that appealed to me. I thought it'd be interesting to spend time with someone who doesn't know my middle name, although the Tin Tin reference caught me quite off guard," Maurice added with a grin.

"Yvonne provided me with yet another justification," he continued. "Last month she mentioned she'd like us to visit friends in Denver. When your letter arrived a few days after her suggestion, it spurred me to google you, not necessarily with the intention of taking you up on your offer, but rather just to see how near to Denver the author of the charming little letter lives."

"When I discovered Denver's not too terribly far from here," Maurice added, "I continued mucking around on the computer. That's one of my hobbies, mucking around on the computer, although some people refer to it as 'wasting time.'"

"I prefer 'mucking around' myself," I added.

"Well, in this instance, my muckings were fruitful, as I began to seriously consider your offer. After more checking on my own, I had Gordon make the site visit. When he came back with a glowing report, minus the bit about the snow, I talked it over with Yvonne. We agreed that Gordon and I should take you up on your invitation. Yvonne and I had already chartered a plane to Denver, so it wouldn't be difficult to drop Gordon and me off in Rapid City on the way."

"So you planned on coming here a couple weeks ago?" I asked.

"Guilty as charged. I apologize for not giving you more than a two-day notice. I know I was taking a chance you might have other plans this weekend. But I didn't want to get your hopes up in case things fell through in the end."

I DIDN'T REMEMBER Nick and Gordon passing us on the trail, but they, along with Shelby, were waiting for Maurice and me on a rocky overlook. After quickly checking for rattlesnakes, we sat down next to them to admire the scenery. From our vantage point, the Harney Peak tower appeared to be miles away. Three rocky ridges and the valleys in between separated us from our destination.

"Don't tell me we're going to make it all the way up there?" Maurice said. He motioned toward the tower with a lit cigarette.

"That's right buckaroo," I answered. "And we're going to have fun doing it, like it or not."

"It's not as difficult as it looks from here," added Nick.

"This is an interesting rock," Gordon said as he inspected a pink stone he held in his palm.

"That's a rose quartz," said Nick. "It's quite common in the Hills. Rock hounds from around the world make pilgrimages to the Black Hills because of its abundance of minerals and fossils."

"What's this sparkly stuff," Maurice asked as he picked up a fist-size chunk of a semi-transparent, shiny substance.

"That's mica," answered Nick. "A composition of gravel and ground-up mica is used on a lot of the trails in the Hills. However, I'll show you an even more useful function."

Nick picked up a piece of mica and began separating the rock into sheets.

"I happen to enjoy flaking off the layers," said Nick. "It's a great stress reliever," he added, intentionally looking my way.

"Years ago, the pioneers used mica as a substitute for glass window panes," continued Nick. "Even before that, Native American's used mica as mirrors."

"That explains why I'm drawn to it," said Maurice as he pretended to preen in front of his chunk of mica.

Then he stood up to stuff the mica in the pocket of his jacket, which the rest of us took as our cue to pick ourselves up off the ground. After I hooked Shelby onto her leash, Gordon, Shelby, and I took the lead for the second leg of the journey.

"Gordon, I really need to apologize to you," I said. "I know I'm directing most of my attention to Mo, but I don't mean to exclude you, even though it may appear that way."

"Don't worry about it," Gordon said. "When you invited Mo, you had no idea I was part of the package. And the way I see it, you're not ignoring me any more than you're ignoring Nick."

"Nick who?" I replied.

"The air smells so fresh and woodsy," said Gordon. "If I lived here, I'd never get tired of the aroma."

"I bet you could even get used to the snow, Gordon," I said playfully.

"I doubt that. Snow is, and always will be a four-letter word. That's an impressive tree," he said as he pointed toward a towering, somewhat uneven evergreen.

"That's a Ponderosa Pine, the most common tree in the Hills. Although they have an irregular shape, they're my favorite tree."

"How did the Black Hills get its name?" asked Gordon.

"The Native Americans call it Papa Sapa," I answered, "which means Black Hills. Since the pine make up about four-fifths of the trees in the Hills, their dark green coloring appears black from a distance. Thus, the name Black Hills."

"Then there's the Black Hills Spruce," I added pointing to a tall, conical tree. "People in the area who cut their own Christmas trees usually prefer Black Hills Spruce because of their even shape."

"I assume you cut down your own Christmas trees?" asked Maurice from behind my shoulder.

"We make a ritual out of it every year," replied Nick. "Usually the first weekend in December, we'll go with a group of friends, all of us in search of the perfect Christmas tree. Sometimes it takes hours. We usually have a contest to see which family finds the best-looking tree."

"Since Nick is so competitive, we usually win," I said. "He's like a man on a mission. The only problem with looking for Christmas trees that time of year, which is the only time most normal people look for Christmas trees, is that it's deer-hunting season. So, we make sure to wear colorful clothing. I even put a splashy bandana on Shelby so she doesn't get mistaken for a deer."

"I'll bet she loves helping you scout for trees," said Maurice.

"I think she likes the outings even more than we do," I answered. "She loves frolicking in the snow."

"How much snow do you get here?" asked Gordon.

"Usually when we look for our Christmas tree, there'll be a couple inches of snow on the ground," answered Nick. "Some years there won't be any. Other years there might be a foot. We're in the middle of a drought right now, so our past few winters have been mild. However, two years ago we got hit with a major snow storm in April."

"That was an experience," I chimed in. "The night before, while Nick and I were packing for a trip to Las Vegas, it was just raining. So, you can imagine our surprise when we woke up the next morning to six inches of snow on the ground, and it was still coming down."

"But we weren't going to let a little snow get in our way," added Nick. "We loaded up the pickup and headed for the airport in Rapid."

"We could only go maybe twenty-five miles an hour," I continued, "because the roads hadn't been plowed yet. When we spotted a snow plow about five miles down the road, our spirits rose, until we realized it was stuck in the snow."

"Not a good sign," said Maurice.

"That's what we thought," said Nick. "So, we reluctantly turned around. By the time we got home, there was close to a foot of wet, heavy snow on the ground."

"And, to add to the thrill of it all," I said, "we lost our electricity."

"And a few hours later, we started hearing what sounded like gunshots," said Nick. "It turned out to be pine tree branches cracking from the weight of the snow. We don't have any pine trees right next to our house because I've cut them all down, but one tree barely missed my outhouse."

"That would have been disastrous," said Gordon.

"Don't you know it," answered Nick.

"I think we counted a total of nineteen trees on the property that had been damaged," I added. "Rather than cavorting around in Las Vegas, we spent the next few days cutting down the cracked trees and burning the slash piles. We ended up working hard during our vacation."

"How long were you without power?" asked Maurice.

"Four days," said Nick. "By the second day the roads were clear, so we were able to drive to Hill City to shower at a friend's house. They invited us to stay with them until our electricity came back on, but we made some lame excuse about having to get back home. We didn't want them to know we actually enjoyed roughing it."

WHEN WE REACHED a valley that was dissected by a small creek, I let Shelby off the leash so she could splash through the water.

"We're half way there, boys," I announced. "But don't get too comfortable. The second half is all uphill."

We crossed the three-foot wide creek courtesy of the rocks that stood in for a foot bridge. Once on the other side, Maurice took special interest in a large boulder that jutted up alongside the path.

"That's granite," I said. "The same type of rock Mount Rushmore and Crazy Horse are carved from."

"Watch it Mo," said Nick. "You want to steer clear of that plant you're about to step on. It's poison ivy."

Maurice comically stepped back from the short, three-leafed plant.

"Not everyone's allergic to poison ivy," said Nick, "but those who are, and who come in contact with it, acquire an awful itch that lasts a few days. I should know. I'm very susceptible to poison ivy. And I've tangled with it more times than I care to admit."

"But they turn a gorgeous red in the autumn," I said. "The Hills don't have quite as many colors as New England in the fall, but we do have our share of autumnal foliage. We have beautiful yellow, lime green, orange, and a splash of crimson."

A young couple approached us on the path. We greeted one another while we continued walking in opposite directions.

"Caroline, I love the way you say 'hey,'" said Maurice. "Is that South Dakota talk?"

"I really don't know," I answered. "Half the time I'm not even aware I'm saying it."

"Well it's charming and if you don't mind, I plan to use it."

When a couple in their fifties approached us, Maurice greeted them with a "hey," complete with a South Dakota accent and a wink in my direction.

"What a beautiful dog," the woman said as she stopped to pet Shelby. Shelby wiggled her butt in delight and then held up her left paw. The woman let out a laugh as she shook Shelby's paw.

"We used to have a red Golden, just like yours. They're such wonderful dogs."

After the couple moved out of hearing distance, I said to Nick, "I'm dreading the day we say those words to an owner of a Golden."

WE PASSED THROUGH an area overgrown with spruce trees. Moss dripped from the branches like dark green icicles.

"This area looks like a forest the headless horseman would call home," said Maurice. "Does anyone ever get lost here?"

"Every year someone seems to get separated from their party," I said. "They're usually found within a couple of hours. But once in a while, they're not discovered until the next day. Even though the temperature during the day can get up to over a hundred, the nighttime temp can be quite chilly. That, coupled with images of mountain lions, and now bears, thank you very much Nick, is enough to keep me from wandering too far from the path."

Chapter 11

ALTHOUGH NUMEROUS SWITCHBACKS helped ease the steepness of the final mile, I asked Maurice and Gordon if they wanted to take a breather half a mile from the summit. To my slight disappointment, since I wouldn't have minded a rest, they said they'd rather wait until we reached the top.

Just below the summit, we walked past a relatively level area.

"There used to be a forest service cabin here," said Nick. "I stayed in it one night during my party days, many years ago. I hiked Harney with three friends late one afternoon. When we got to the summit, we smoked a little weed and then took part in some extreme rock climbing. That was during my invincible days when I didn't know the meaning of fear, if you know what I mean."

"I went through that stage once or twice," said Maurice.

"We brought our sleeping bags with us because we were planning on sleeping at the top. But it was a lot colder than we expected, so we decided to check out the cabin. Fortunately for us, the forest service caretaker had left a note on the door stating that said campers were welcome to stay in the main room of the cabin if they didn't disturb his belongings."

"Quite a generous chap," said Maurice.

"At the time we really didn't appreciate his hospitality as much as we should have. The cabin was fairly small. Realtors would call it cozy. There was a bedroom, a tiny bathroom, and a combination kitchen and living room. The caretaker came in after we had eaten our supper of beef jerky and granola bars. He greeted us warmly and then retreated to his bedroom while the four of us camped out in the living room. We must have stayed up half the night because the caretaker had to ask us to keep it down a few times. But the next morning, he graciously made us a breakfast of bacon and eggs. I think we gave him some money for his generosity, at least I hope so."

"What happened to the cabin?" asked Maurice.

"The forest service razed it a few years later because too many people were vandalizing it."

FINALLY, WE APPROACHED a series of steep stairs that led to the summit. Nick and I let Maurice and Gordon take the lead. When Maurice reached the top landing, a few exhausting minutes later, he instinctively bent over to catch his breath. Once he realized he had reached the summit, he straightened up and took his first view.

"What a magnificent sight," exclaimed Maurice. "Caroline, you never told me how breathtaking this would be and I mean that literally," he said as he continued to breathe heavily.

Gordon was breathless and speechless.

"We can get an even better view from Harney's highest point," Nick said.

He led us to the entrance of the rock tower. We climbed the tower's narrow, metal staircase while Shelby waited at the base of the stairs.

"Would you look at this view," Maurice said.

We gazed at the rolling sea of hills, trees, and rock formations that surrounded us.

Maurice recorded the scenery while I added commentary.

"On a clear day, you can see five states from here." I pointed to the south. "There's Nebraska, at the far edge of the southern Hills. Wyoming's to the west. To the northwest is Montana. On the clearest of days you can even see North Dakota. And to the east, you can see the grasslands of South Dakota. There's Rapid City," I said, pointing to a shiny area at the northeastern foot of the Hills. "Where the prairie meets the Hills."

"See that rock formation," Nick said. He pointed to a large granite formation roughly seven miles to the northeast. "That's the backside of Mount Rushmore."

"Where is it?" asked Maurice still filming.

"Move the camera to the left a little," instructed Nick. "That's it."

"Now pan the camera to the right a bit," said Nick.

"Got it," said Maurice. "What am I filming now?"

"The pigtails, that's where Caroline got sick yesterday," answered Nick.

"Nicholas," I exclaimed.

"What?" said Nick. "I'm just helping Mo capture memorable moments from this weekend."

"And I appreciate your thoughtfulness, Nick," said Maurice.

"LET'S GET OUT on the granite," I suggested. "I like the view from the rocks better than from the tower."

We carefully climbed down the stairs and greeted a group of people as they waited to take our place in the tower. Shelby then led us outside to a narrow set of rock steps. We followed her to the face of a massive granite boulder that overlooked the northern Hills. We situated ourselves on the boulder.

Apart from the sound of Shelby slurping up water in her portable dish, we sat in silence for a few minutes taking in the scenery and enjoying the rest.

Maurice was the first to break the silence.

"This is so peaceful. What a wonderful place to meditate, to put everything into perspective."

"I've been up here more than a dozen times," I said. "But I never get tired of sitting here and letting my mind wander."

"I feel like I'm at the top of the world," said Maurice as he took a puff from his cigarette.

"The Lakota consider Harney Peak to be the center of the world. Have either of you heard of the book *Black Elk Speaks?*" I asked Maurice and Gordon.

"Actually, my dear," said Maurice, "I've been paging through the book the past couple of nights."

"You have?" I asked.

"I found it in the bookcase in my room. It looked interesting, so I started skimming through it and, before I knew it, I'd more or less gone through the entire book."

"That's Mo for you," said Gordon. "He's so full of surprises."

"You usually say I'm full of something else," responded Maurice.

"True," answered Gordon. "So, what's this book about?"

"From what I can recall, Nick Black Elk—I remember his first name because it's also the name of one of my gracious hosts—Nick Black Elk was a holy man from a local Tribe."

"The Oglala Sioux, also known as Oglala Lakota," I added.

"That sounds about right," continued Maurice. "*Black Elk Speaks* is his autobiography, as told to a professional writer. Black Elk's son acted as interpreter since his father spoke Sioux and not much English. In the book, Black Elk talked about the coming of the Whiteman."

"Wasichu." I pronounced the word as wuh-SHE-chew.

"So that's how you say it," said Maurice. "I was racking my brain trying to figure out how to say Wasichu every time I came across it. Anyway, Black Elk talked about the life of his people, visions he had for their future, and how he feared their lifestyle would ultimately be destroyed by the coming of the Wasichu."

"One of his visions," I added, "which occurred when he was just nine years old, took place right here at the top of Harney Peak. Although he wasn't physically here, Black Elk gained insight into the sacredness of life and the role he hoped to play to bring about more harmony to the world."

"That's one reason," said Nick, "that this part of the Black Hills is called the Black Elk Wilderness area."

"When was the book written?" asked Gordon.

Maurice tilted his head toward me.

"Probably in the early 1930s," I answered. "And I think Black Elk was born in the early 1860s."

"Sounds like he lived an incredible life," added Maurice. "As a young warrior, Black Elk actually fought in the Battle of Little Bighorn. Custer's Last Stand."

"Later in his life," I added, "he was also at the Wounded Knee Massacre, which is where I personally think his spirit was more or less broken."

"And he talks about Crazy Horse in the book," said Maurice. "Weren't the two related?"

"I think they were second cousins," I answered.

"Talk about being related," said Maurice, "I also have a connection to Black Elk."

"This I gotta hear," said Gordon.

"When he was in his twenties, Black Elk performed in Buffalo Bill's Wild West show in New York City and then eventually onto Europe. He joined the show because he wanted to learn all he could about the ways of the Wasichu in order to ultimately help his people. So, while he was in England, Black Elk and a couple of his friends got left behind in Manchester for a couple of days."

"Didn't you live in Manchester when you were young?" asked Gordon.

"Precisely, Watson. I plan on eventually doing my own detective work into Black Elk's adventures in Manchester. See if I can map out where he went and what he did in my old stomping grounds."

"You do know," added Maurice, "that if someone would have told me three months ago that I'd be spending time in South Dakota, I would have called them more than crazy. Funny what a change of scenery can do for a person. I've gone to new heights this weekend. In more ways than one."

WE SAT IN silence again for a few minutes, soaking in the view until my stomach began to rumble.

"Anyone else hungry?" I asked.

I rummaged through the backpack. "We have beef jerky, trail mix, cheese sticks, granola bars, and dog biscuits. Any takers?"

Shelby quickly took up my offer for dog biscuits and the humans snatched up the remaining goodies.

Somewhere in the vicinity a telephone rang. Maurice retrieved his cell phone from his jacket's inner pocket.

"Hello? Well hello, Yvonne," Maurice said as he stood up. "You called at a good time. You won't believe where I'm at. . . I can't wait to show you the footage I shot today."

Maurice nodded to us before he walked away to continue his conversation.

"You two are really lucky to live here," said Gordon. "I had no idea South Dakota has so much to offer."

"Especially if you're into outdoor activities," I said.

"We make good use of the forest service trail system," added Nick. "We have a couple of four-wheelers that take us to places most people don't even know exist. I wish you were staying another day. We'd take you and Mo on some of our favorite trails."

Maurice approached us as he finished his conversation with Yvonne. "I'll see you tomorrow. . . Love you too."

"Yvonne says hello to all of you," said Maurice. "She says she's having a good time in Denver. But I get the feeling she'd rather be here with us."

"Maybe next time," I said.

"That's a possibility. Hey, Caroline. How would you like to talk to Robin? I'll give him a ring, see if he's home."

"Where's he at? Florida? England?" I asked trying to mask my anxiety. When Barry called unexpectedly yesterday, I didn't have time to get nervous. But now I could feel my heart pounding in my chest.

"He should be at his home in England," Maurice answered as he punched a few numbers on his cell phone.

"Hello, this is Maurice, is Rob there? . . .Sure." After a brief pause, Maurice said, "Hello dear brother. . . Guess where I'm calling from? . . . No, I'm not in England. . . I'll give you a hint, the Wild West. . . Nope, not even close. I'm in South Dakota and right now I'm standing on the highest point between the Rockies and the, uh," he paused.

I whispered, "the Pyrenees."

"Between the Rockies and the Pyrenees, north of the Tropic of Cancer. Can't forget the Tropic of Cancer. I'm on Harney Peak. And wait until I tell you about our connection to Black Elk, a Lakota holy man. Gordon and I got here on Friday. . . We'll leave tomorrow. . . No, she's in Denver. We're here as guests of Caroline and Nick Nichols. . . I'll tell you the whole story later. I'm having a blast, Robin. We went to Mount Rushmore yesterday. . . Right, the four presidents. Pictures don't do it justice. The only way to see it is in person. Oh, and we saw the Crazy Horse carving. There's a Native American museum on the grounds you'd go mad over. . . I saw buffalo yesterday. . . No, I didn't pet one. I didn't care to get gored. . . Oh, and Caroline and Nick have a log house. . . It's gorgeous, they built it themselves. I'll be sure to take pictures. . . The closest city is

Rapid City, but I've been spending the entire weekend in the beautiful Black Hills of South Dakota. The air is so fresh here. . . I can't really say right now. . . Yes, do you want to talk to Caroline? . . Just say hello. . . Hold on a second."

Maurice handed the phone to me and said, "Robin wants to say hello."

"Hello Robin. This is Caroline Nichols."

"Hello Caroline," replied Robin, shyly. "Sounds like Maurice is having quite an adventure."

"My husband Nick and I are having quite the adventure ourselves."

"Please forgive my unfamiliarity, but where are the Black Hills?" asked Robin.

I was prepared to give him a stock answer, but decided on an alternate approach.

"Well, on the road to Alaska they're just north of Nebraska," which prompted a thumbs-up gesture from a nearby Maurice.

"Something tells me you're familiar with our music," Robin said with a chuckle.

"*To Whom it May Concern* includes one of my favorite songs of yours, 'Never Been Alone.'"

"That's kind of you. Not too many people mention 'Never Been Alone.'"

"Well more people should, it's beautiful."

My nervousness propelled me to continue talking. "Robin, what's your weather like today?"

"Well Caroline, it's a typical day in England, it's overcast and rainy. How's the weather in South Dakota, which is just north of Nebraska?"

"Oh, it's about sixty-five degrees with beautiful blue skies and not a cloud in sight. A perfect day for sightseeing. But we really could use some of your rain."

"I'll send some over your way. Anything else you need?" asked Robin.

"Thanks, the rain should be enough."

Then my impetuous side got the better of me. "You know Robin, there is something else you could do for me. However, I'll understand if you decline. Could you sing a couple bars of 'I Started a Joke' for me?"

"Only if you understand that I haven't exercised my vocal cords today, so it may sound like rubbish."

"I'll take that chance."

I heard him clear his throat. "Here goes," he said before he began to sing.

"I started a joke. . ."

"You got me started," he said after singing the first verse. "Hope you don't mind if I go on."

Of course, I didn't mind. Then he continued in his stunning voice.

"I started to cry. . ."

I lip-synced perfectly throughout the entire song.

"That was beautiful Robin, just beautiful. Thank you so much. It's not every day a Bee Gee serenades me over the phone. Wait, I forgot. Yesterday, Barry sang to me over the phone."

With mock disgust Robin said, "How dare he. Who was better?"

"I'll never tell," I replied. "Robin, how would you like a souvenir from the Hills?"

"Sure, Mount Rushmore would make a smashing addition to my garden."

"Granted, I did get Mo to come to the Black Hills, but I'm not a miracle worker by trade. How about something with a Native American theme?"

"Only if you make Mo pay for it."

"It's a deal. I've really enjoyed talking with you Robin. And thank you again for the song."

"It's been my pleasure."

Chapter 12

WE TOOK ONE last look at the magnificent view before we began our descent. Nick talked Maurice and Gordon into taking the little-known shortcut, which bypassed the switchbacks we trudged up almost an hour earlier.

The shortcut began with a climb down a large outcropping of steep granite rocks, which Maurice and Gordon accomplished with minimal difficulty. When we reached the bottom, I told them to turn around.

"You mean to tell me we climbed down that wall of rock," proclaimed Maurice. "I can now add rock climbing to my list of accomplishments."

"You're in great shape," I said.

"Go ahead, you can say 'for a man of my age,' all of fifty-two," said Maurice.

"Well you look and act ten years younger," I said. "You're definitely in better shape than I am. How do you keep fit?"

"My new passion is paintball."

"You mean where you shoot people with paint?" I asked.

"That's a simplified description, but yes," said Maurice.

"Call me ignorant but I thought just teenage boys were into paintball," I said.

"It's a fantastic sport and far more difficult than you'd imagine. I picked it up again last year and quickly became obsessed. I'm even on a team. So's Gordon."

"How often do you play?" asked Nick.

"At least once a week," replied Maurice. "Even more when we're practicing for a tournament."

"Aren't you going to tell them about your paintball shop?" said Gordon.

"You own a paintball shop?" asked Nick.

"I opened it about a month ago. The grand opening's in a few weeks."

"I'm impressed," said Nick as he and Maurice exchanged a high five.

"What's it called?" I asked.

"Commander Mo's Paintball Shop."

"Why Commander?" I asked.

Maurice looked at Gordon and they both grinned.

"Because the Queen of England has appointed me and Barry and Robin to be Commanders of the Order of the British Empire," Maurice answered unable to mask his pride.

My mood turned serious. Not knowing exactly what to do in the presence of a Commander, I politely curtseyed in front of him.

Maurice waved me off and said, "That's not necessary, Caroline. It's very kind of you, but it's not necessary."

"How long have you been a Commander?" I asked.

"Since the beginning of the year," replied Maurice.

"What exactly is a Commander of the British Empire?" asked Nick.

"It's one of the highest honors the Queen grants to those deemed to have given exceptional service to the Crown," answered Maurice.

"Congratulations, Mo," I said.

"Do you know what I am now?" he added mischievously. "A CBE Bee Gee."

OUR CONVERSATION CEASED as everyone's attention turned toward inching down a steep, rugged path of rocks and pine needles.

Nick finally broke the silence when we neared the bottom of the hill.

"Believe it or not, this route used to be a jeep trail that led to the cabin just below Harney's summit. When the Forest Service banned motorized traffic to Harney back in the sixties, they dumped these boulders on the road to discourage anyone from using the path. Now the only people who take this route are the ones who know about it and are willing to take a chance of breaking an ankle on the way down."

"That was wise of you," said Gordon, "not to mention the broken ankle part until just now."

WHEN OUR SHORTCUT joined up with trail number nine, we met a couple in their forties who were headed toward the summit. I hooked Shelby back to the leash while everyone exchanged greetings. As we continued down the path, the couple lingered at the fork for half a minute before jogging back our way.

"You're one of the Bee Gees, aren't you?" asked the woman breathlessly.

"Yes I am," replied Maurice.

"I told you, Jimmy," said the woman. "Which one are you? I know you're not Robin or Barry."

"I'm Maurice, love," he replied graciously.

"Right. I knew that. I love your music. I can't believe you're here. Are Robin and Barry here too?" she said.

"Sorry, they're back home."

"That's all right. Could I take your picture, Maurice? Jimmy, you did remember to bring the camera, didn't you?"

"You can take my photo only if you're in the picture, too," Maurice said as Jimmy took off his backpack and rummaged around for the camera.

"I can take a picture of the three of you," I offered.

"Are you Maurice's wife?" the woman asked.

"I wish. No, this is my husband," I said as I pulled Nick to my side.

"Caroline and Nick, and Gordon here, are friends of mine," said Maurice.

After I finished off a roll of film, I handed the camera to the beaming woman.

"Thank you, Maurice. And say hi to Barry and Robin for me."

"I will, it's been my pleasure," replied Maurice.

"I SEE THAT grin on your face," said Maurice, as the two of us walked side by side down the trail. "What are you thinking about?"

"About how classy you are. You were so charming to that woman even though she couldn't recall your name but remembered Barry and Robin's. I don't think I would have been nearly as friendly."

"If you only knew the old me, back when it really annoyed me when Barry and Robin would get more attention. Since I rarely sing lead, people think I don't contribute as much. But through the years, as I've become more comfortable with myself, I realize what other people think isn't as important as I once thought."

"Why don't you sing lead on more songs?" I asked with more bluntness than I had intended.

"If Robin and Barry didn't have such striking voices, I probably would sing lead more often. As luck would have it, I rather enjoy singing harmony, finding just the right notes that add a unique texture to a song. And I have this knack for arranging music. So, there's not much time left to sing lead."

"Plus, I assume the number of instruments you play is also a factor."

"Yes, I normally use that excuse as well," said Maurice with a grin.

"So, what's your favorite instrument?"

"That's a much harder question than you'd think since I've never met an instrument I didn't like."

"Like the Mellotron?" I asked.

"Ah yes, the mysterious Mellotron. The Beatles introduced me to it when we were working on our first British album."

"You played it on 'Every Christian Lionhearted Man Will Show You,'" I added. "What a terrific song."

"One of our more avant-garde songs."

"It's so creative, I just love it. Your songwriting abilities just floor me."

"To be honest,'' said Maurice, "sometimes they floor me, too."

"It wasn't until I took piano lessons in my early teens," I said, "that I even thought about the songwriting component of music. One day I played a Carole King song on the piano for my teacher. He asked if I owned any Carole King records. When I said yes, he said my assignment for the week was to listen to those records, keeping in mind that she wrote or co-wrote all of her songs. I really didn't know what he was getting at, but listening to music sounded much more appealing than practicing scales."

"So, throughout the week," I continued, "I played my two Carole King albums. After a few days, I think when I was listening to 'Tapestry,' I finally understood what my teacher was trying to get through to me. Hope I'm not boring you."

"Do go on," said Maurice. "I love hearing about people's experiences with music."

"Good answer. Well during my next piano lesson, we talked about the bond composers have with their songs. I think we even listened to a couple of Neil Sedaka songs as examples. My teacher promised that if I took the time to explore the meaning of a song, and even pretend that I wrote it, I'd be able to play the song with more spirit, more oomph."

"Did it work?" asked Maurice.

"Surprisingly, yes. And I was hoping my new-found respect for composers would rub off on my own songwriting endeavors. But it didn't in the least. Whenever I tried to write songs, they all ended up sounding like the Campbell's soup song. I couldn't come up with an original tune, which is why I'm so impressed with your songwriting skills. I wish I had a tenth of your talent. I assume it's something you were born with."

"That and a good mentor. As youngsters, Robin and I were quite fortunate because Barry would write songs so effortlessly we saw no reason not to have a go at it ourselves."

"How old were you when you wrote your first song?"

"Probably five or six, but it was a nonsensical little tune. One of my proudest moments as a young composer was at sixteen when I wrote my first song we recorded as a group. It was called 'Where Are You.'"

"I don't think I've heard it," I said.

"Not too many people have," laughed Maurice. "We recorded it while we were still in Australia."

"Can you sing some of it for me?" I asked.

"I haven't sung it in years. I don't think I even recall the words," said Maurice.

As we continued hiking down the trail, Maurice started to sing under his breath. Then he began singing out loud.

"Where are you. . ."

Apparently, he did remember the words because he continued to sing the upbeat, early sixties-style song.

"Our love would grow. . ."

When he finished he gave me a big grin and said, "Guess I remembered it after all. Believe you me, I've written better songs since, but I don't think I did a bad job the first time around."

"You really enjoy performing, don't you?" I asked. "That twinkle in your eye grew even brighter when you were singing."

"I suppose I do. Particularly in front of a live audience. By the way, flattery will get you everywhere."

"Do you ever get stage fright?" I asked.

"No, not stage fright, but I do get nervous beforehand. Praying the equipment doesn't malfunction, hoping the audience will connect with our performance. But once we get on stage, my worries quickly fade and I'm able to thoroughly enjoy the show."

WHEN WE APPROACHED the creek at the half-way point, I let Shelby off the leash to allow her to enjoy the creek in ways that only dogs can, while her two-legged friends crossed the creek by means of the stepping stones.

"So, how did you and Nick meet?" asked Maurice as we continued down the trail.

"While we were at college. We both went to South Dakota State University. That's east river."

"East river?" asked Maurice.

"Sorry, east of the Missouri River, which is also known as the Mighty Mo. Of course I consider you to be the original Mighty Mo."

"Thank you for the clarification," said Maurice.

"The Missouri River," I continued, "basically cuts South Dakota in half. I grew up on my parent's farm, east river. Nick and I both went to SDSU and hung around in the same group, although we never dated each other. He graduated a year before me, so I lost track of him until we bumped into each other in Rapid one day, shortly after I graduated. We dated for four years before I finally proposed to him. Not that I'm pushy. . ."

"No, I can't imagine," said Maurice.

"Okay, you've been around me long enough to realize I can be assertive. But when I know what I want, I go after it. There's nothing wrong with that, is there?"

"No, it's a very admirable trait. Plus, if I said any differently, you'd probably hit me."

Maurice unsuccessfully dodged my playful punch to his left arm. He clutched his left shoulder in mock pain.

"You coulda been a contenda," Maurice said in a decent Marlon Brando impersonation.

"So how long has Nick been under your thu . . . I mean, how long have you and Nick been married?"

"We just celebrated our fifteenth wedding anniversary. And they've been fifteen very happy years."

"Haven't they Nick," I shouted to Nick who, along with Gordon, was a couple dozen paces ahead of us.

"What ever you say, dear," replied Nick.

"I love you too," I shouted back.

"How long have you been married, Mo?"

"It'll be twenty-seven years this fall. I can't believe Yvonne's put up with me for that long. To tell you the truth, I think we're both happier now than we've ever been. The last eleven years have been the best. That's how long I've been sober," Maurice added with a serious tone.

My tongue was tied because I wasn't expecting him to bring up his alcoholism at that moment.

"Don't worry, Caroline," said Maurice. "I don't mind talking about my drinking. It actually helps with my recovery."

"I thought you said you were cured?" I answered.

"No, I'm sober, but not cured. I am, and always will be, a recovering alcoholic."

"How old were you when you started to drink?" I asked.

"It began innocently enough when I was in my late teens, when the three of us were being accepted into the British music scene. Back then I drank to socialize. And I'd go clubbing with the best of them. Eric Clapton, Ringo, David Bowie, Keith Moon, Rod Stewart. I was on the fast track and I had no intention of stopping because I was having the time of my life."

"I won't bore you with all the years in between," continued Maurice. "But I will tell you about the turning point, which was the day I hit bottom. I was at the lowest point a person can possibly go mentally, emotionally, physically, even spiritually."

"Somehow I came to the huge realization that my life would continue on this downward spiral unless I took steps to change it. That was in 1991 and I've been sober since. My life has never been better."

"Is it hard to stay away from liquor?" I asked cautiously. "Do you ever get the urge to drink?"

"I haven't for a while now, but I never let my guard down. Fortunately, I have family and friends who support me. Plus, I attend AA meetings of some form or another every single day."

Maurice noticed the quizzical expression on my face.

"You're probably wondering how I've fit in AA sessions the past couple of days. Gordon's part of my AA group. I'm actually his mentor. The two of us have already held a few impromptu sessions this weekend."

"You have?" I asked.

"I have a confession, Caroline."

Maurice kicked at a small stone on the path.

"This entire weekend is more or less a therapy session. Gordon and I thought it'd be a good idea to get away from our regular surroundings and find out how strong we've become. Gordon hasn't spent a night outside of Florida since he joined AA. I thought he was ready to stretch his wings. This weekend is as much of a self-assessment for Gordon. . . and for me, as it is a mini holiday. I hope you're not offended, but in essence, we're using you and Nick."

"If course I'm not offended, Mo. I'm honored."

Chapter 13

WHEN WE REACHED our starting point near Sylvan Lake, I checked my watch. "Three hours and twenty-five minutes. Not bad, especially since we spent close to forty-five minutes at the top."

"I thought the high altitude might slow you two down," said Nick, "but apparently it didn't. How do you feel?"

"My feet are a tad sore," answered Maurice. "Other than that, I feel great."

"My hamstrings are a little tight," Gordon said as he propped his right foot on a tree trunk and leaned forward. "But nothing a good stretch can't cure."

"Gordon, do you mind if I let Shelby take a swim in the lake?" I asked. "I'll dry her off with a blanket before I put her back in the Land Rover."

As if on cue, Shelby walked over to Gordon and lifted her left paw.

"Go ahead and shake hands with her Gordon," said Maurice. "She won't bite."

As Gordon reached out to take hold of Shelby's paw, Maurice said. "I forget Gordon, Shelby's a dog. She might bite," which prompted Gordon to back away.

"I'm kidding Gordo," laughed Maurice. "Shelby wouldn't hurt a fly."

While Gordon cautiously shook Shelby's paw, Maurice leaned toward me and whispered, "She wouldn't hurt a fly, would she?"

I whispered back, "She eats flies."

"Gordon," said Nick, "why don't you throw a stick in the water and let Shelby retrieve it? Here, I'll show you."

Nick picked up a stick and flung it hard enough to splash in the lake forty feet from the shore. Shelby dove into the lake as soon as the stick left Nick's hand. She deftly paddled toward her target, grabbed it with her teeth, and swam back to Nick.

"Watch out everyone," I warned as Shelby emerged from the water and shook herself off, spraying water in all directions.

"Thanks for the shower, Shelby," said Nick. "But I did have one earlier today."

Nick took the stick from Shelby and handed it to Gordon. "Go ahead and throw it."

Gordon's pitch landed near Nick's throw.

"Look at her go," said Gordon. "She's a good swimmer."

"Thanks to the swimming lessons she took as a pup," I said.

"She didn't take lessons, did she?" asked Gordon.

"Obedience lessons, yes, but swimming lessons, no. Golden's are naturally good swimmers. They should be. They have webbed feet."

"Sorry Caroline, you're not going to get me this time," replied Gordon.

"No, really. I'll show you."

Once Shelby got out of the water and shook herself off, I made her lay on her side.

"See, Gordon," I said as I lifted up one of her front paws. "It's webbed."

"It is webbed. I thought you were pulling my leg again."

"I thought you were, too," said Maurice. "Let me have a look."

Shelby lay patiently as Maurice inspected Shelby's front paws and then her back paws. "I've even owned

Golden's and I didn't know they had webbed feet. You're part duck, Shelby."

Maurice picked up Shelby's stick and threw it in the water. Shelby jumped up and ran to the edge of the water before making a beautifully executed dive into the water.

"The Soviet judge gives her a perfect ten," Maurice announced with a Russian accent.

Shelby would have retrieved the stick for as long as the pitchers were willing, but I could tell she was tiring quickly so I got her blanket from the Range Rover. She raced toward me when she noticed the object in my hands. A rub-down was an even bigger treat than retrieving sticks.

After her towel drying session, Maurice and I walked with Shelby to the far side of the lake to give her a chance to dry off more, while Gordon and Nick met us on the other side via the Range Rover. When Gordon opened the back of the vehicle, Shelby willingly jumped in and, after tucking her stuffed cow under her chin, settled down for a nap.

"That's the gift shop I was telling you about, Mo," I said, pointing to a woodsy-looking building at the edge of the parking lot. Maurice and I ventured inside while Nick and Gordon sat on porch chairs made from willow tree branches.

"Robin mentioned he wanted you to bring him back something with a Native American theme. How about a star quilt?" I asked as I pointed to a display of beautiful Native-American quilts.

"Good idea," said Maurice. "They're gorgeous."

I wandered through the store while Maurice pondered over which quilt to buy for Robin.

"Hey Mo, you and Gordon need to get these," I said as I held up a t-shirt that proclaimed, 'I Climbed Harney Peak' underneath a drawing of the summit.

"Absolutely," answered Maurice.

"Here, let me hold Robin's quilt so you can pick out shirts for you and Gordon."

While he searched through the display of t-shirts, I paid for Robin's star quilt as well as three others for Maurice, Barry, and Gordon. When Maurice was content with his selections, he brought the t-shirts to the register and warmly greeted the cashier.

"Are you from England?" she asked.

"Originally, yes."

"I thought so. I love British accents," she said as she rang up the t-shirts.

"Did you forget to add in the quilt?" asked Maurice.

"She already paid for them," the cashier said as she nodded in my direction.

"Them?" exclaimed Maurice.

"We can talk about it outside," I said as I carried two over-sized sacks out the door.

"Let me do this," I said walking across the porch. "They really weren't that expensive."

"What do you mean by they?" asked Maurice as he took one of the sacks off my hands.

"Well, I also bought a star quilt for you, and Barry, and Gordon."

"Caroline, what am I going to do with you," Maurice said. "Thank you for your generosity. But, I'm not through with you yet. At least I can give you something in return straight away, modest though it may be. I bought shirts for you and Nick, too."

Maurice presented me with a dark green t-shirt.

"Gordon, we have ultimate proof that we trekked Harney Peak," Maurice said as he threw dark blue t-shirts to Gordon and Nick.

"Let me guess," said Gordon. "You got a black one for yourself."

"You are psychic, Gordo," Maurice said as he held a black t-shirt up to his chest.

"I love black," Maurice said to me.

"You look good in it. Why fool with perfection."

"My sentiments exactly," said Maurice.

WE ATE A leisurely lunch at the Sylvan Lake Lodge half a mile from the lake before driving home to drop off Shelby.

Chapter 14

A SMALL, YELLOW car with a black roof greeted us when we pulled into our driveway a half-hour later.

"That's a Mini Cooper," I exclaimed. "Nick, do you know anyone with a Mini Cooper?"

"I don't even know what a Mini Cooper is," answered Nick.

I jumped out of the Range Rover and sprinted toward the car. "Are you expecting any visitors, Mo?"

"No, but I was expecting this car. It's ours to use for the rest of the weekend. I thought a Mini would be fun to tool around in. Something tells me you approve."

"I love Minis," I said as I peered in the window.

"My first choice was an Aston Martin," said Maurice, "but the one I favored only seated two."

"Plus, Astons are hard to come by in South Dakota," I added.

"That wouldn't have stopped Gordon. He's the one who found the Mini," said Maurice.

After I put Shelby in her outdoor kennel, we all freshened up enough to feel confident about riding in a small vehicle with three other people for much of the afternoon. Maurice then took his place behind the steering wheel. I claimed the passenger seat, which left the roomy back seat for Gordon and Nick.

"I haven't driven a Mini in years," Maurice said as we reached the end of the driveway. "This should be an adventure."

With that, he stepped on the gas, pulled onto the highway, and we zipped north in high fashion.

"This bugger has power, doesn't it?" said Maurice. "Good choice Gordo. Caroline, I'll rely on you to be my navigator."

"Oh no," replied Nick. "We'll probably end up in Canada."

I turned my head to sneer at Nick before I said to Maurice, "Just stay on this road. It'll take us right into Deadwood. The only things you need to watch out for are deer, and I'll keep my eyes open for them as well."

"I love to drive," said Maurice, "especially on winding roads like this."

The posted speed limit was fifty-five, but Maurice kept it around a respectable sixty.

Five miles from our house, Nick pointed to a lookout tower in the distance. "That's the Seth Bullock tower, named after Deadwood's first sheriff. The lookout is used to spot forest fires."

"Do you get many fires?" asked Maurice.

"Two years ago, the Jasper fire burned over eighty-thousand acres in the southern Hills," answered Nick. "It was the biggest fire ever recorded in the Hills. Luckily, it was in a fairly remote area, so only a summer cabin and a few outbuildings were destroyed."

"Even though the fire was more than ten miles from our house," I said, "I started packing, just in case."

"It's been dry the past few years," added Nick. "So we could be in for another bad fire season this year. But it's a risk we think is worth taking. Look, we're at Pactola already. This is where I caught the trout we ate last night."

On the left-hand side of the road, a dark-blue lake with an irregular shoreline, inhabited by towering ponderosa pine, attracted our attention.

"Yet another gorgeous lake," Maurice said as he pulled into the visitors' center parking lot. "I need to capture this on film."

Nick and Gordon headed for the visitor's center while I followed Maurice to the railing that overlooked the lake. Maurice shot footage of a small sailboat gliding across the water before moving the camcorder in my direction and asking me what I knew about the lake. I dodged the camcorder so he would pan back to the water.

"This is Pactola, one of the largest man-made lakes in the Black Hills. The town of Pactola was located in this valley before Rapid Creek was dammed in the late fifties, to provide water to the growing community of Rapid City and the nearby base, which is now called Ellsworth Air Force Base."

Maurice stopped filming and said, "People around here have a habit of turning towns into lakes, don't they?"

"So much so," I answered, "that we've learned not to cuss out a town or someone might take it literally. Damn that town! Yes, sir. We'll get right on it!"

Maurice inhaled a deep breath of pine-scented air and said, "Everything smells so fresh." He then lit a cigarette. "Seems like a contradiction, talking about fresh air and then lighting one up."

"I love being near water," continued Maurice as he leaned against the railing. "It seems to energize and relax me at the same time. On the days we're recording at our studio in Miami Beach, I'll take my lunch at a nearby park that overlooks the Biscayne Bay. It's my little retreat where I can watch the antics of the seagulls and get hypnotized by the water. Every once in a while, I lose track of time and someone from the studio has to get me since I don't carry my cell phone when I go to the park. I can just imagine their conversations back at the studio, 'Where's Mo?' 'Bet he's probably feeding his birds again.' 'I'm worried about that one. Think he's off his rocker.'"

111

"'Whose turn is it to go get him this time?'" I said in a baritone voice.

"'I think he purposely forgets just to rile us up,'" added Maurice.

"And do you ever?" I asked.

"Me? Never," answered Maurice.

"Do you want me to film you in front of Pactola, Mo? You really do need to be in a few of your pictures, otherwise no one will believe you were here. They'll roll their eyes and say, 'Right Maurice. I believe you were in South Dakota.' Under their breath they'll say, 'Must have been feeding the birds again.'"

WE WEREN'T BACK on the road more than five minutes before I quickly pointed to the right-hand side of the road.

"Watch out Mo," I said. "A deer's about to jump up on the road."

As Maurice slowed down, the deer darted across the road, narrowly missing the front of the Mini.

"That was close," said Maurice. "Thanks for taking your job as navigator seriously."

"We can usually spot most of the deer before they're about to run across the road. But not always. I've hit a couple of deer throughout the years. So has Nick. Depending on their size, they can do a lot of damage."

"Talking about doing some damage," said Maurice, "I think that calls for a few rounds of a little game I call Name that Car Tune. Turn on the radio and the first one to guess a song's title and artist wins that round. Do I have any takers?"

"You know I can't pass up the challenge," I said.

"I've never been good with song names, so I'll just be a bystander," replied Nick.

"You'll be joining us sooner or later, you'll see," said Maurice. "How 'bout you Gordon, You'll humor me, won't you."

"It's the other way around, Mo. You humor me."

Two seconds after Maurice turned on the radio, he blurted out, "'Wild Thing,' the Troggs."

"No fair," I said as the song's introduction played in the background. "I didn't know we were starting yet."

"All's fair in love and music," replied Maurice. "Caroline, once someone guesses correctly, hit the seek button and let it go on to the next station. By the way, is this AM or FM? It'll give me a better idea of the type of songs we're listening to."

"I just switched it to FM," I said, "but I don't think you need any help. Okay, everyone ready? Let the games begin."

". . . of weathered sand . . ."

"'Yellow Ledbetter.' Pearl Jam," I answered a split second before Maurice.

"I see we have a real competitor on our hands," said Maurice.

". . . I'll protect you . . ."

"'Blurry' by P.O.D.," I spit out.

"Wrong answer," said Maurice. "It's Puddle of Mudd, not P.O.D. Amateurs often make that mistake."

"Ouch, that hurt," I said.

". . . with two cats. . ."

"'Our House,' Crosby, Stills, Nash, and Young," Maurice answered.

"Are you sure it's not Crosby, Stills, and Nash, minus Young?" I asked.

"Positive," answered Maurice. "God, they had great harmony, with or without Young. Or should I say, they *have* great harmony since they're touring again. Caroline, I assume you know what 'Our House' is about."

"Graham Nash wrote it after a morning outing with Joni Mitchell," I said.

"Correct. And around that same time, Stephen Stills wrote a song for his love interest. What was it and who was she?" asked Maurice.

"He wrote 'Suite Judy Blue Eyes' for Judy Collins."

"Correct again. Well done. But, I'll bet you didn't know Stephen played percussion on one of our songs. A little tune called 'You Should Be Dancing.'"

"Actually, I did know that," I answered. "Courtesy of the *Children of the World* sleeve. But I thought Stills just played guitar."

"If you're in a band, you often play more than one instrument, for a couple of reasons. One, you have more artistic control. And two, the main reason I may add, is you don't have to pay for more musicians, which is particularly important when you're first starting out."

"How did Stills end up playing on 'You Should Be Dancing?'"

"Back when we recorded it in '76, it was common for artists to sit in on one another's recordings. Strum a few bars on the guitar, lay down some percussion tracks. I did it a few times myself. The day we recorded 'You Should Be Dancing,' Steve was taping in a nearby studio. He stopped by to say hello since he and Barry used to chum around together, and he ended up sitting in on the song."

"Every so often I have to pinch myself to remind me of the company I'm keeping this weekend," I said. "You're so down to earth that it's easy to forget just how accomplished you are. Does it ever seem like your life has been a dream?"

114

"Sometimes it does all seem surreal," replied Maurice. "I do think how incredibly lucky I've been."

"Talented, not lucky," I said. "Speaking of which, this morning you were talking about your success in Australia. But didn't your big breakthrough occur when you moved back to England?"

"It did. We eventually left Australia because we wanted more exposure. Ironically, on the boat trip over, 'Spicks and Specks' hit number one in Australia. For a split-second we thought about returning to Australia, but we knew we owed it to ourselves to have a go at it in England."

"How old were you then?" I asked.

"It was the beginning of 1967, so Robin and I would have been sixteen."

"That's incredibly young," I said. "So you had a record contract lined up in England before you left Australia?"

"No, we didn't. We staked the future of the entire family on our dreams of making it big in England, scary as it may seem. But we weren't totally unprepared. Before we left Australia, we sent tapes to the Beatles' Brian Epstein. Apparently Brian handed them over to one of his colleagues, Robert Stigwood. Not long after we arrived in London, Robert got a hold of us and the rest is history."

"At least you didn't have to go knocking on doors," I said.

"We did a bit of that before Robert contacted us. And we still had to audition for him. I can remember that day as if it were yesterday. We thought we had performed well enough, but Robert didn't seem impressed. We left the session feeling absolutely miserable. But later in the day, we got word that Robert wanted to sign us to a contract after all."

"So, he had liked your audition?" I said.

"He had been impressed by the tapes we sent and couldn't wait for us to arrive in England. We didn't know it at the time, but the audition was just a formality. We misread his lack of enthusiasm at the audition as apathy. We quickly learned that Robert doesn't wear his emotions on his sleeve. As it turned out, we were just what he needed at that point in his career. And he was just what we needed."

"Around the time we were getting ready to record our first album," continued Maurice, "Robert thought it would be a good idea to add a couple more musicians to the group to make it a proper band. Back in Australia we used to jam with drummer Colin Peterson and Vince Melouney, who played lead guitar. When we discovered they were both in London and were looking for work, we hooked back up with them. It turned out to be a nice fit."

"I always thought the Bee Gees were just the three brothers," said Nick.

"We'd like to think we could do it all on our own, but particularly with the number of sounds we incorporate into our music, we need to have a core group of musicians, especially when we perform live. Of course, Colin and Vince aren't with the Bee Gees anymore. They were with us for just the first few albums. The musicians we have now, who've been with us for years, are as much a part of the Bee Gees as Barry, and Robin, and I are."

"You're being modest," I said.

"No, I'm not known for my modesty. Gordon can attest to that. I'm just being honest."

"So, what was it like recording your first British album?" I asked. "Were you nervous at all?"

"Other newcomers might have found it frightening or overwhelming, but not us. We'd been preparing for the moment ever since we began singing together. So, for us it was an amazing time. We wrote all new songs for the album, which didn't take long. While we were recording, Robert was busy lining us up for guest spots all over England. So immediately after we finished the album, we began appearing on TV shows and radio programs. By the time our first single 'New York Mining Disaster' hit the air, the Bee Gees were fairly well known throughout Britain."

"I remember when 'New York Mining Disaster' was released," I said. "For my eighth birthday, my parents gave me a transistor radio, which was my constant companion all summer long. 'New York Mining Disaster' happened to be one of the songs I'd turn my radio up for that summer. And I remember being so concerned about the fate of the men trapped underground. My mom had to explain to me that no one was trapped in a mine and that people make things up when they write songs."

"Hate to break it to you, Caroline," said Nick, "but you're still pretty gullible."

"Sorry to disappoint you, Nick," said Maurice, "but 'Mining Disaster' was loosely based on actual events."

"I knew it," I said triumphantly. "That explains why I still get chills whenever I hear it. What a great song for your first big hit. Did it go to number one?"

"Although millions of other people also turned their radios up for 'Mining Disaster,' it got close but didn't quite make it to the top."

"What was your first number one?" I asked.

"'Massachusetts,' which hit number one in England."

"How'd it do in the States?" I said.

"It went to eleven."

"You'd think it would've done as well, if not better, since the song's set in the U.S.," I said.

"I'd be a rich man if I could predict how well our songs would fare," said Maurice.

"You are a rich man, Mo," remarked Gordon.

"What was your first number one in the States?" I asked.

"'How Can you Mend a Broken Heart,' which didn't even chart in the UK. That was in '71, the year after we got back together."

"You split up?" asked Nick. "Why'd you do that?"

"We got tired of each other, Nick. We needed our own space. Up to that time, the three of us had never been apart. We did everything together, well almost everything," Maurice added with a grin. "Robin was the first to leave."

"What'd he do then?" I asked.

"He put out an album that produced the number two song, 'Saved by the Bell.' So, he did rather well. In the meanwhile, Barry and I released the *Cucumber Castle* album under the Bee Gees name. And, ironically, our single 'Don't Forget to Remember' also climbed to number two. But shortly afterwards, Barry and I agreed to go our own ways."

"What'd you do during that time?" I asked.

"I actually kept rather busy. Lulu and I were newly married, so she rightly occupied much of my time. Since she was touring quite a bit then, I'd travel with her some. We'd take amazing side trips to the far corners of the world. Other times, Lu's brother, Billy, and I kept ourselves out of trouble by writing and recording music. We wrote quite a few songs together, including radio and TV commercials."

"What else did I do?" continued Maurice. "I arranged and produced music for other artists, including Tin Tin. If you can believe it, I even acted in a West End musical called *Sing a Rude Song*. I can admit now that I wasn't a great actor. Hell, I wasn't even a good actor. But I had a fabulous time."

"Did you ever think about pursuing acting further?" I asked.

"Even though I got caught up in the excitement of the theatre and would have liked to try more acting, I could never stay away from music for any period of time. Fortunately for the stage world, Barry, Robin, and I got back together shortly after my stage debut."

"How long were the three of you apart?" Nick asked.

"Almost two years. Strangely enough, when we got back together, we realized the separation was the best thing that could have happened to us. By being apart, we proved we didn't need each other to survive. When we got back together, we realized how much we missed each other's company and missed working together. I enjoy writing songs by myself, but it doesn't compare to writing with Barry and Robin. The three of us feed off of each other. It's hard to explain, but when we write a song together, we get such a rush. It's like a natural high really. . . I'm sorry I keep dominating the conversation."

"Go ahead and dominate," said Nick. "I could listen to you for hours."

"And you know me, Mo," added Gordon. "I never get tired of your stories. Plus, I've learned more about you this weekend than I have in the past two years since I've known you."

"And if you don't mind," I said, "I want to hear more about your relationship with Barry and Robin. Are the three of you really as close as you seem to be?"

"We don't spend as much time together as we used to since we space our records out more these days and we have our own families that keep us busy. But, although Barry's three years older than Robin and me, we often feel like triplets. That's how close we are. It helps that we truly enjoy each other's company."

"I assume you and Robin have a special bond since you're twins," I asked.

"Even though we're not identical twins, we couldn't be any closer."

"Do you like being a twin?" I asked.

"For the most part I really do. It's comforting knowing you have this special connection to someone else. However, I haven't known any differently. Do you enjoy being a non-twin, Caroline?"

119

"Point well taken, Mo," I said. "But to tell you the truth, I've always wanted to be a twin."

"I didn't know that," said Nick.

"Growing up as an only child on a farm can be very lonely," I said. "I used to have an imaginary friend who was my twin. We used to play games together and gossip and share jokes. My mom was pretty worried about me at the time. I overheard her telling my dad that she was thinking of taking me to see a therapist. But my dad convinced her that it's natural for children to have imaginary playmates and that I would outgrow it."

"Did you?" asked Nick.

"I'm not telling."

Chapter 15

WE PARKED THE Mini Cooper in a secure location and began our tour of Main Street Deadwood.

"So, this is the infamous Deadwood," announced Maurice. "Gordon, we've made it to the Wild West."

"It's gotten even wilder now that you've arrived," said Gordon.

"Caroline, what can you tell us about Deadwood?" asked Maurice.

"Nick knows more about the town than I do. He used to live here when he was young, so I'll let him tell you anything and everything you want to know about Deadwood."

"I'm not so sure about that," said Nick. "But is there anything in particular you want to know?"

"Wasn't Wild Bill Hickok killed in Deadwood?" asked Maurice.

"You know your history, Mo," said Nick. "Hickok moved to Deadwood in 1876 to work a mining claim during the big gold rush in the Hills. Before he came to Deadwood he had been a marshal in a couple of towns in Kansas and had built up quite a reputation as a marksman, an ambidextrous one at that."

"He was also quite the gambler," continued Nick, "so he fit in nicely in Deadwood. Whenever he played cards, he liked to sit with his back to the wall, so he could keep an eye on everyone who came in and out of the saloon."

"One fateful day in August, just a few months after he arrived in Deadwood, Hickok went to Saloon No. 10 to play poker. Unfortunately, he couldn't oust the person who was sitting in his regular chair. So Hickok had to sit with his back to the door. Soon enough, a good for nothing named Jack McCall slithered into the saloon and shot Hickok in the back of the head, killing him instantly."

"Why'd he do that?" asked Gordon.

"No one's really sure," answered Nick. "Some say he was seeking revenge because Hickok killed his brother in a Kansas gunfight. Others say Hickok embarrassed McCall in a poker game the night before. Even others say McCall was part of a larger conspiracy to eradicate Hickok."

"When he died," said Maurice, "wasn't Hickok holding a poker hand that became known as the dead-man's hand?"

"Yes he was," answered Nick. "He was holding a pair of aces and eights."

"Hickok is buried at the Mount Moriah Cemetery here in Deadwood," I added. "If we have time we'll take you there. Buried next to him is Calamity Jane."

"I've seen the movie *Calamity Jane* more times than I can count," said Maurice. "So, I've always wondered whether the two could actually have been romantically involved."

"It is possible," answered Nick. "There are so many different versions of Calamity's life that it's hard to tell fact from fiction. However, the one undisputed aspect of her life was her love for Hickok. Some say Calamity was Hickok's mistress or even his wife. Others claim it was one-sided love and that Hickok cringed whenever he saw Calamity. If that's the case, he probably turned over in his grave when she was buried next to him, apparently at her request."

"Once I had . . . ," Maurice started to sing.

"I love 'Secret Love' sung by Doris Day," I said. "The song's about Calamity Jane's crush on Hickok," I said to Gordon and Nick.

"I just thought of something, Mo," I added. "Since you seem to be such a fan of Calamity Jane, was the Bee Gees' song 'Secret Love' inspired by the 1950s 'Secret Love?'"

"It's hard to say. When you write a song, you grab onto ideas that are floating around in your head at that particular moment in time. Although our song isn't about unrequited love, parts of it, including the title, could have been inspired by the earlier song."

"THERE'S SALOON NO. 10," Gordon said pointing to a sign across the street.

"That's not the original site of the bar," said Nick, "The first Saloon No. 10, which was located a block or so from here, burned down in 1879, along with most of Deadwood."

"Let's get something cold to drink inside the reincarnated Saloon No. 10." I said.

A waiting line outside the bar is a perpetual fixture on Friday and Saturday nights. However, we had no trouble finding an unoccupied table on this Sunday afternoon.

Maurice and Gordon took in the Old West feel of the place, despite the slot machines. A cocktail waitress dressed like a saloon girl asked if she could get us anything.

"Howdy, Miss Kitty," said Maurice. "Bet no one's ever called you that before?"

"You're the first one today, cowboy," she answered with a wink.

"Do you want to try a sarsaparilla?" Nick asked Maurice and Gordon. "It's similar to root beer." As an afterthought he added, "There's no alcohol in it."

After receiving a "sure" and "why not," Nick ordered a round of sarsaparillas.

"I'm sorry," I said. We should have checked with the two of you before we brought you into a bar. We don't have to stay."

"Don't worry about us," said Gordon. "We wouldn't have come in if we didn't feel comfortable."

When Miss Kitty returned with four sarsaparillas, Nick slipped her money so quickly that Maurice didn't even have time to reach for his wallet.

"You have got to be the quickest draw in the West, Nick," said Maurice as he pulled some money from his wallet and tried to reimburse Nick.

"Thank you, but no," said Nick. "You and Gordon are our guests. I have to admit I'm enjoying myself a lot more than I thought I would. When Caroline finally convinced me that you and Gordon were going to spend the weekend with us, I was a bit apprehensive. I thought you'd feel uncomfortable and then we'd feel uncomfortable. But I'm the first to admit when I'm wrong, and in this case I'm happy to admit I was way off base."

"I knew we'd get along famously," said Maurice.

"I don't know anyone who doesn't get along with you, Mo," said Gordon. "You've got to be the most amiable person I know."

Maurice lifted his mug and said, "Cheers to good friends."

"Cheers," we repeated as we clinked our mugs together in midair.

Chapter 16

BEFORE LEAVING SALOON No. 10, we all donated a few dollars to the quarter slot machines.

"How long has Deadwood had gambling?" asked Maurice as we walked down Main Street.

"It was legalized around 1990," I said. "Deadwood was struggling at the time, so gambling helped to revitalize the town. Nick and I aren't big gamblers, but we still enjoy coming up here every once in a while, especially on holidays when they go all out. On St. Patrick's Day, Deadwood turns into Dublinwood. On Halloween it's Deadweird, and on New Year's Eve it's a heck of a lot of fun."

"I assume those are mannequins in the windows," said Maurice. He pointed to scantily clad figures in the second-floor windows of the casino across the street.

"Ladies of the evening are no longer permitted in Deadwood," said Nick. "But, brothels were common during the gold rush days. And although prostitution became illegal in Deadwood, probably in the 1940s, it was still openly practiced here up until the 1980s."

"Openly practiced, behind closed doors," I added.

"Speaking of the law," said Nick. "Remember the Seth Bullock lookout tower I pointed out near Pactola? The hotel we're standing in front of was built by Bullock. He followed the gold rush to Deadwood to open a hardware store. Shortly after Wild Bill Hickok was killed, the proper people of Deadwood thought it was time to bring structured law enforcement to town. Bullock, who had been sheriff of

Montana Territory before he moved here, accepted the position as Deadwood's first sheriff."

"Around the turn of the century," Nick added as he held the front door open for us, "he built this hotel, which now doubles as a casino."

"Apparently he still enjoys his hotel," I said. "A number of guests have reported seeing the ghost of Seth Bullock in the hotel."

"Is this a picture of Teddy Roosevelt?" asked Gordon as he pointed to one of the many century-old pictures hanging on the casino walls.

"It is," said Nick, "And the man standing next to him is Bullock. They first met while Roosevelt was Vice President. They soon became good friends and remained so until the end of their lives."

"When Roosevelt would visit Deadwood," continued Nick, "Bullock liked to take him to a peak outside of town that had an impressive view of the hills. In fact, the peak was eventually named after Roosevelt. When Bullock heard of Roosevelt's death in January of 1919, Bullock, along with help from a local society club, built a stone tower atop Mount Roosevelt to honor his friend. Roosevelt Tower, also called Friendship Tower, was completed just before Bullock died in September of the same year."

"What a charming story," said Maurice.

"Get a load of this," I added. "At the time that Bullock would take Teddy up to the peak, Teddy owned a ranch in southwestern *North* Dakota. I don't know how true this is, but legend has it that Teddy could actually see his North Dakota ranch through binoculars atop Mount Roosevelt."

"Now that's taking drastic measures to check up on the ranch hands," said Maurice. "Oh, talk about checking up, I promised Barry I'd call him today, let him know what he's missing out on, including Mount Roosevelt."

"I'll meet you all outside," Maurice said as he located his cell phone and headed out the front door.

126

WHEN THE THREE of us exited the Bullock Hotel a few minutes later, we found Maurice surrounded by a group of admirers. He was enjoying himself as he signed autographs and joked around with fans.

"Does he ever worry that someone might attack him?" I asked Gordon.

"He takes prudent precautions when necessary. But for the most part, he'd rather live a normal life than have to worry about the 'what ifs.'"

Maurice's entourage quickly grew once word spread of his presence in Deadwood. Gordon caught Maurice's eye and communicated with him through hand signals.

"You two stay here," said Gordon. "I'll be back in a few minutes."

While we waited, Nick and I crept closer to the crowd.

"Have you gone to Mount Rushmore yet?"

"Disco sucks. But I still have my *Saturday Night Fever* album."

"Is this your first visit to Deadwood?"

"When are the Bee Gees coming to the Civic Center? Neil Diamond performed there."

"You are so handsome in person."

"Are Barry and Robin here, too?"

"You're one of my favorite bass players."

"Brenda, move in closer. I want to get you in the picture, too."

A few minutes later, a dark green SUV driven by Gordon pulled in front of the Bullock Hotel. Gordon waved Nick and me over to the driver's door.

"We'll meet you two by the Mini Cooper in a couple of minutes," said Gordon. "We'll switch vehicles there."

Then he whistled at Maurice.

"Sorry, I have to leave soon," said Maurice. "My ride is here. Did everyone get an autograph who wanted one?"

After a few more minutes of picture taking and autograph signing, Maurice excused himself with genuine sincerity. He hopped into the waiting SUV and waved to the crowd as Gordon drove off.

"Sorry it took so long," Gordon said when he and Maurice arrived at the parking ramp a few minutes after Nick and me. "We had to take a few detours on the way to the garage."

"You *are* good Gordon," I said as we assumed our designated seats in the Mini Cooper.

Maurice paused just before turning the key and said, "I'm being selfish. Does anyone else want to have a go at driving the Mini?"

I was more than eager to get behind the wheel, and I had a feeling Nick and Gordon felt the same. But the three of us turned down his offer. We could tell Maurice was thoroughly enjoying his stint as driver.

"Gordon, do you or Nick want to sit up front?" I offered. "I'll change seats if you do."

"You better stay up there, Caroline," said Nick. "We'll be traveling on a winding road."

"I knew motion sickness was good for something," I replied.

A DRIVING TOUR of Lead was next on our itinerary.

"The towns of Lead and Deadwood are located so close to each other," said Nick, "that locals often refer to them collectively as Lead-Deadwood."

"Lead is home to one of the largest gold mines in the world," continued Nick, "or should I say *was* home. The great Homestake Gold Mine just closed its doors at the end of 2001 because it wasn't profitable anymore. See that large open cut area to the right? That's where two brothers discovered the Homestake mother lode back in 1876, during the gold rush madness. A year later, they sold their claim to an individual who owned a number of mining interests in the country. You might have heard of him, George Hearst."

"The name's vaguely familiar," said Maurice.

"Most people are more familiar with his son, William Randolph Hearst, the publishing mogul," said Nick.

"And even more people," I added, "are familiar with one of William's granddaughters, Patty Hearst."

"Wasn't she the one who was kidnapped in the seventies?" said Maurice.

"Wasn't that an odd event," I said.

"Truth is often stranger than fiction," said Maurice.

"Anyway," said Nick, "back during the gold rush days, Lead and Deadwood were complete opposites even though they were just three miles apart. Deadwood was a town of gambling and saloons and brothels and gunfights. Lead, on the other hand, offered libraries and opera houses."

"Sounds like a great combination," said Maurice. "Spend Sunday through Wednesday in Lead and Thursday through Saturday in Deadwood. The best of both worlds."

ACTING AGAIN AS navigator, I directed Maurice to the outskirts of Lead and toward the city of Spearfish.

"To the right are a couple of ski resorts," I said, "They're not the Rocky Mountains, but they do nicely."

"I assume you two ski," said Maurice.

"We used to downhill ski almost every winter weekend," replied Nick. "But now, to avoid the lines, we either take an occasional day off during the week or go cross country skiing on the weekends."

"Isn't it time for another round of Name that Car Tune?" I asked as I turned on the radio.

". . . to the bank. . ."

"Toby Keith. 'My List,'" said Maurice. "Switch to the AM band. Let's try out our skills there."

". . . you love me."

"'A Lover's Concerto,' by the Toys," said Maurice, "which was based on a minuet by. . ."

"Bach," I said. "I know my music, Mo."

We came upon a small community, located at a fork in the road, that consisted of a lodge and a combination convenience store and gas station.

"This is Cheyenne Crossing," said Nick. "Gordon, I have a feeling this is the last place you'd like to be in the winter. Cheyenne Crossing gets some of the highest snow totals in the Hills. It's perfect snowmobile country."

"I don't understand," said Gordon, "why anyone would voluntarily spend time outside in the snow. That's why I moved to Florida from Baltimore after high school. By the way, did I thank you yet for waiting until spring to invite Mo to the Hills?"

"THIS STRETCH OF road we're on goes through Spearfish Canyon," said Nick, "one of the most scenic drives in the Hills, especially in the fall. You'll like it Mo, it's full of twists and turns."

"Let's see if the Mini Cooper's up to the challenge," said Maurice as he shifted into sixth gear.

"Let's see if you're up to the challenge," I said as I pressed the seek button on the radio.

". . . say no. Hold . . ."

"'Tracy' by the Cuff Links," I said.

"Your answer will only count if you respond correctly to this follow-up question," said Maurice. "I believe 'Tracy' was the only song recorded under the Cuff Links name. However, the fellow behind 'Tracy' was involved in another musical endeavor that hit the charts the same year, 1969. What was that song and what was the name of the group?"

"I have no idea," I said. "I'll guess 'Where my Rosemary Goes' by Edison Lighthouse."

"Wrong answer, but an excellent guess, Caroline. Let me tell you why. The lead singer for Edison Lighthouse used to be in a group called The Flying Machine, which released the hit 'Smile a Little Smile for Me.'"

"Rosemarie," I sang to prove I knew the song.

"He must have liked the name Rose," said Nick.

"Why's that?" I asked.

"You know, Rosemary goes, Rosemarie," answered Nick.

"And you say you don't know music," said Maurice. "So any other guesses to my Cuff Links question? No? The correct answer is 'Sugar Sugar' by the . . . ."

"Archies," I answered. "You mean Archie and Betty and Veronica and Jughead . . ."

"Don't forget Reggie," said Gordon.

"And Reggie didn't sing 'Sugar Sugar?'"

"Sorry to burst your bubble," said Maurice.

"I loved the Archies," I said. "My main reading material when I was in grade school was Archies' comic books. Now you're telling me my idols couldn't sing. Come to think of it, when I used to watch their Saturday morning cartoons, I could swear they were lip syncing. This explains it."

"Mo?" I asked. "What are your thoughts on lip syncing, especially during concerts?"

"For some performers, and the fans who attend their concerts, the music isn't the main attraction. To them the dancing and light shows are just as important as the music. When you're dancing nonstop for an hour and a half, it's very difficult to sing. Some performers can do both, but not everyone."

"Have the Bee Gees ever danced on stage?" I asked.

"No, thank God. We want to keep the audience in the arena. In order to pull it off, all three of us would have had to dance. Since none of us particularly likes to dance, or can dance, the idea never seriously crossed our minds."

"Which is so ironic," I said, "since most people associate the Bee Gees with disco."

Chapter 17

WE PASSED A sign announcing our arrival in the small community of Savoy.

"Mo, you might want to take the next turn," said Nick. "I want to show off Roughlock Falls to you and Gordon."

Maurice turned left at the Savoy lodge and drove another mile and a half before reaching the fall's picnic area.

As we got out of the Mini Cooper, I asked, "Did either of you see *Dances with Wolves*?"

"Sure."

"Of course."

"Most of the movie was filmed on the prairie east of Rapid," I said. "But remember the closing scene with the snow-covered hills? When Kevin Costner and Mary McDonnell's characters leave the Tribe? That was filmed right here."

"Look," Nick exclaimed as he pointed toward a large bird circling overhead. "That's a bald eagle."

Maurice lifted his camcorder to film the impressive, white-headed bird as it soared above our heads. He kept the camcorder rolling as we strolled toward the Roughlock Falls trailhead. We paused on the footbridge that crossed Spearfish Creek to watch the water as it playfully tumbled over the rocks in its path and to take in the adjoining scenery produced by wildflowers and the aspen, spruce, birch, and pine trees.

"There's a mile-long trail to the falls themselves," said Nick. "Do I have any takers?"

"You three can go without me," I said. "I must have pulled a hamstring during this morning's hike."

"If you don't mind, I'll stay here with Caroline," said Maurice. "The blisters on my feet are begging for a rest."

Gordon was eager to see the falls, so he and Nick took to the trail while Maurice and I moved to a picnic table next to the creek to watch a mother duck and her ducklings paddle around in the water. Meanwhile, two tame squirrels approached us, hoping we'd offer them food. The duo scampered away once they realized we didn't have as much as a crumb between us.

Although I'm usually not one to keep thoughts to myself, I hesitated before I spoke next.

"Mo, do you mind if I ask you about the Bee Gees and their link to disco?"

"Of course I don't mind. And if you don't mind, I'd like to hear why you stopped listening to us then."

"Fair enough and I'll even begin. When *Saturday Night Fever* came out, I was the first in line to buy the album. My college roommate and I practically wore it out. I swear *Fever* was a stable on my turntable for a year and a half. But the fall of '79, when I began working at the college radio station, the deejays were bashing disco with a passion. I confronted them initially because I'd seen most of these guys at the local disco just four months earlier dancing to music from the Bee Gees, Donna Summer, the Stones, Paul McCartney, Blondie, et cetera, et cetera. But something happened over the summer to change their minds."

"Comiskey Park comes to mind," said Maurice.

"Exactly. I remember watching the news accounts the night it happened. . ."

"July of 1979," said Maurice.

"I'll take your word for it. When I first heard that a Chicago radio station was hosting a disco record-burning session during halftime at a ball game, I thought it'd be a harmless dig at disco. But when I watched the news footage, I was amazed at how quickly the scene turned mean spirited and violent. It was a text-book example of the mob-effect theory."

"We didn't expect anything as harsh as that to occur," said Maurice, "although we had braced ourselves for a backlash. You can't fly as high as we were flying for that long without having someone try to shoot you down."

"Didn't the Bee Gees hold something like the top five spots on the charts around that time?"

"Songs we composed held five of the top ten spots on Billboard in early '78," said Maurice.

"I can think of three right off the bat," I said. "'How Deep is your Love,' 'Stayin' Alive,'' and 'Night Fever.'"

"The other two were Samantha Sang's 'Emotion' and Andy's 'Love is Thicker than Water,'" added Maurice. "And we followed *Fever* with another extremely successful album, *Spirits Having Flown*. We were the darlings of the American airwaves for almost two straight years."

"So how did you handle the backlash when it came?"

"Not very well at first, I admit. I was particularly frustrated at what I considered fickle American radio stations. How dare they overplay our songs and then blame us for the flood of Bee Gees music on the air."

"What was the scene like overseas?" I asked.

"The radio stations most everywhere else were much more kind."

"How did you feel about your former fans that joined the attack on disco, present company included? Like I was alluding to, I more or less stopped listening to your music shortly after I began working at the station. Out of the dozen or so deejays, I was the only rookie and the only female, a highly impressionable one at that. When the guys continued to bash disco music, including the Bee Gees, I thought since they had worked in radio longer than I had, they must know more about music than I did. So I quietly went along with them."

"What was most annoying to me at the time," said Maurice, "was that people would let radio stations, and the media in general, totally influence their listening habits. At first the stations were pushing disco, so that's what the public bought into. Then when the stations bashed disco, the public followed suit, no questions asked."

"The Bee Gees never considered themselves a disco band, did they?" I asked.

"No, we actually don't like to label our music, whether it's pop, rock, R&B, adult contemporary—let alone disco—because we cross so many different lines."

"Did you ever get death threats from disco haters?" I asked.

"Plenty, ninety-nine point nine-nine percent of which we didn't take seriously. But there were those few that caused me to look over my shoulder more than I would have liked."

"Do you want to hear my theory on why the disco backlash occurred?"

"Absolutely," said Maurice.

"When disco went mainstream, women flocked to the night clubs to dance to this music with the great beat. Well men had no choice but to follow them. Even though most of these guys hated to dance—probably because they couldn't—they ended up on the disco floor every weekend, performing what Billy Crystal's Harry Burns referred to as 'the white man's overbite,' because they knew dancing was their best bet at scoring. Once they got wind of disco bashing, they eagerly joined in."

"I'm sure there's some truth to your theory," said Maurice. "You could do a whole study on the rise and fall of disco. In fact, some people have. But I honestly wouldn't have changed a thing. We reached a level of commercial, even critical, success that most bands only dream about."

"Your disco music defined a period in history," I added.

"Precisely. I'm not bitter in the least about the disco backlash. I can even laugh about it now."

"All the way to the bank?" I asked sheepishly.

"All the way to the bank," laughed Maurice. "There's no doubt about it. The money was fantastic. Especially when you consider that just before the disco era, we were performing in small clubs because we hadn't scored a hit in years. We were still releasing records, but apparently not the type the public wanted to hear."

"You didn't ever consider quitting the music business, did you?"

"Never. Never crossed our minds. We were determined to come back stronger than ever."

"Which you did thanks in part to your falsettos."

"In a way, yes. In 1974 we hooked up with a producer who helped us find our rhythm-and-blues style. Our first major album using R&B was *Main Course*, which also happened to be one of the first times Barry sang falsetto. The three of us had so much fun experimenting with this new sound that we started writing songs to showcase it."

"Could you sing a little falsetto for me right now?" I asked.

"It's actually much harder than you'd imagine," Maurice said as he stood up. "But sure, I'll have a go."

"Tragedy, when you..."

Maurice sang the first verse of "Tragedy." Then without missing a beat, he lowered his voice two octaves and sang the chorus to "The Lord."

"You can believe. . ."

"You're amazing," I said as I gave him a hearty applause.

Maurice reciprocated by bowing gracefully.

"So," I continued, "around the time you incorporated falsetto into your music, disco started appearing in the mainstream . . ."

"And the falsetto seemed to fit right in with disco music," said Maurice. "We've done dozens of non-disco songs with the falsetto, but when people hear the word falsetto, nine times out of ten they think of the Bee Gees and disco music."

"So once disco fell out of popularity," I added, "so did the Bee Gees because people still connected you with disco."

"Yes, which led to yet another speed bump in our career. But again, we kept busy. We decided since radio wouldn't play our music, we'd go behind the scenes and write and produce for other artists."

"That was a smart move," I said.

"It was a practical move, actually. We weren't about to sit back and watch the world pass us by. Besides writing and producing for Andy, we spent much of the eighties writing for Barbra Streisand, Diana Ross, Dionne Warwick, and Dolly Parton and Kenny Rogers."

"And writing hits at that," I added

"Yes, many of them did turn out to be hits. And we were thrilled to be a part of their success. Barry produced Barbra's album and sang a few duets with her including 'Guilty,' which the three of us wrote. 'Guilty' ended up reaching number one all over the world and the album became her best seller."

"I assume you were also pleased with Kenny and Dolly's success with 'Islands in the Stream.'"

"'Islands' turned out to be one of the best-selling country and western songs ever. That aside, I was thrilled Dolly wanted to record a song we had composed, particularly since she's such a gifted songwriter and lyricist. The next time you listen to one of her songs, pay close attention to the words."

"I remember in the mid-seventies," I said, "when Dolly was crossing over from country to pop. At first I thought, 'Who is she to think she can do both? She's either country or she's pop.' I quickly recognized that not only was she ambitious, but she was also talented. I'm not much of a country music fan, but she's helped me appreciate it more."

"Not everyone in South Dakota listens to country music?" teased Maurice.

"No and we don't all drive pickups either," I answered.

"You have a pickup, don't you?"

"Yes, but that's beside the point," I laughed. "So, was it hard to have other people record your songs?"

"It was incredibly hard. It was almost like having your baby taken away from you and given to someone else to raise. But we were realistic about the situation. We knew that Bee Gees music wouldn't get a warm reception on the radio, particularly on American stations."

"Did it make it easier or harder when those songs turned out to be big hits for other artists?" I asked.

"Easier, no question. We always have and always will consider ourselves songwriters first and foremost. So, we were thrilled our songs did so well. Of course, the artists' performances had something to do with the success of the songs. Dionne did such a wonderful job with 'Heartbreaker.' She turned out to be a wonderful surrogate mother. All of them did, really. Even Kenny."

Chapter 18

A FEW MINUTES after we were back on the road to Spearfish, Maurice exclaimed, "Did you see that?"

"What? Another deer?" I answered as Maurice steered the car around and drove back toward an old hydropower plant.

"The sign on that building. It said Maurice."

"Oh, that's right. This is the community of Maurice," said Nick, pronouncing the name as Muh-REES. "The power plant here used to provide electricity to Homestake's mining operations."

"Are you sure it's not pronounced Morris?" said Maurice as he parked the car in front of the plant.

"I guess I don't know for sure," answered Nick.

"Then there's only one way to find out, isn't there?" said Maurice as he hopped out of the Mini Cooper. "Let's go ask."

"The plant isn't operating anymore," said Nick.

"No, I mean go ask the people who live here." Maurice motioned toward the three houses within walking distance of the plant.

"You are crazy, Mo," I said.

"Of course I am. I'm surprised it took you so long to figure that out. But first I want to get a picture of my name sake."

After I filmed Maurice in front of "his" sign, the four of us walked to the house nearest the plant. When we reached the front yard, Nick stayed behind while Maurice, Gordon, and I strolled up to the front porch.

Images of a shotgun-toting hermit ran through my mind as Maurice knocked on the screen door. I was relieved when a friendly-looking man in his early seventies answered, and my stomach growled when an inviting aroma drifted our way.

"I'm sorry to intrude on your Sunday afternoon," said Maurice. "But my friends and I were driving through the area when we noticed the unusual name of your hamlet."

"Who is it, Joe?" asked a female voice from the back of the house.

"Some tourists asking about Muh-REES," answered Joe.

Maurice turned toward Gordon and me and frowned.

"Would you like to come inside?" asked Joe.

"That's very kind of you, but we don't want to impose," said Maurice. "Plus, you've already answered my question. I was wondering whether your town is pronounced Morris or Muh-REES."

"It depends who you ask," said the woman as she walked toward us, wiping her hands on her apron. "Joe says Muh-REES, but I prefer Morris. Why do you ask?"

Maurice flashed Gordon and me a big smile before saying, "Because my name is Maurice, spelled just like the town."

"Now isn't that something. It's nice to meet you, Maurice. I'm Gertie and this is my husband, Joe," she said as she stepped outside. "If you're not going to come in, we'll take a breather with you and your friends here on the porch."

I gestured for Nick to join us.

Maurice shook Gertie and Joe's hands and introduced Gordon and me. "And the bashful lad coming up the lane is Nick."

"We bought this place back in 1967, wasn't it Joe," said Gertie as she motioned for us to have a seat on the porch.

"The spring of '68," corrected Joe. "Remember, that's the year we bought the Barracuda Fastback."

"You're right. And that was also the year we celebrated Angela's sweet-sixteen birthday up here. We had a house in Rapid City at the time. But we bought this cabin because we wanted a place in the Hills where we could relax on weekends. This is our permanent summer residence now. The rest of the year we live in Phoenix, not far from Angela and the girls."

"You caught us at a good time," said Joe. "We just came back from Arizona last weekend."

"When we moved here," said Gertie, "all the locals pronounced the name as Muh-REES. But Angela called it Morris. It sure made them angry. Being the troublemaker that I am, I started calling it Morris, too," laughed Gertie.

"They almost got us kicked out of here," said Joe.

"I can't even remember now why Angela called it Morris," said Gertie. "No, I do remember. It had to do was a rock group she liked. One of the member's names was spelled like Muh-REES but was pronounced Morris."

The four of us stole glances at each other, which resulted in an exchange of smiles.

"Angela begged us to buy this place just because of the name. She said it was fate. Angela loved their music. She practically listened to it every waking hour."

"I hated it," said Joe. "It sounded like noise."

"Everything sounds like noise to you except for Gene Autry," replied Gertie.

"True," agreed Joe.

"I actually liked their music," continued Gertie. "And every once in a while, I still hear their songs on the radio and I think back to our early days here at the cabin."

"Do you remember the name of the group?" asked Maurice.

"No, but I think I still have a stack of Angela's 33s. Let me go check. I shouldn't be long."

Gertie went in the house and rummaged around in a closet for a few minutes before she came back outside clutching an armful of albums to her chest.

"I knew I hadn't thrown these out. Angela would never have forgiven me."

Gertie flipped through the albums.

"The Turtles, no. The Monkees, no. The Who, no. Simon and Garfunkel, The Beatles, Paul Revere and the Raiders, The Rolling Stones, The Supremes. None of these."

"Sounds like a three-ring circus to me," said Joe.

"This is the group," Gertie announced as she held an album out in front of her. "The Bee Gees. I remember now."

"Weren't they nice looking young men," she said before handing the album to Maurice.

"Especially the chap on the left," said Maurice.

"I couldn't tell you which one Maurice was though," said Gertie.

"I believe it was this one," Maurice said as he pointed to the chap on the left.

"You were a fan of their music, too?" asked Gertie. "What a small world. I wonder what they're doing now."

"Well, the nice looking one is sitting on your porch, Gertie," said Maurice trying unsuccessfully to hide a smile.

"He's what?" said Gertie. "I don't understand."

"Gertie, we have a Bee Gee on our porch," said Joe.

"Oh my goodness!" Gertie exclaimed as she jumped up from her chair. "This is wonderful. I can't wait to tell Angela. She'll be so thrilled."

"No, she won't," said Joe. "She'll be upset she didn't come back with us this weekend."

"Joe, go get the camera. I want to take some pictures. Do you mind, Maurice?"

"Not if you don't mind me taking some of you," he said holding up his camcorder.

After the photography session, Gertie asked if we had eaten supper yet. Maurice replied that we were planning to catch a bite in Spearfish.

"I just made a big batch of my famous white chili," said Gertie, "and we would be offended if you didn't share it with us."

Maurice received eye confirmation from the three of us before he answered, "Well, we couldn't offend you now, could we. Plus, your chili smells heavenly, Gertie."

As it turned out, the chili tasted even better than it smelled. We followed the main course up with homemade rhubarb pie.

"So, where are you all from," asked Joe. "Maurice, are you from England?"

"Originally yes. Now I live in Florida. So does Gordon."

"Can I make anyone some tea?" asked Gertie. "I know how the British like their tea."

Maurice was the only one who accepted her offer.

"Where do you two live?" Joe asked Nick and me.

"Near Sheridan Lake," I replied. "We're showing off God's country to the Floridians this weekend. We just came from Lead-Deadwood and Roughlock Falls."

"Did you show them the Thoen Stone at the Adams Museum?" asked Joe while Gertie poured hot water over Maurice's tea bag.

"We had to make a quick exit out of Deadwood, so we didn't have time," said Nick.

"What's the Thoen Stone?" asked Maurice.

"Only one of my favorite subjects," said Joe as Gertie rolled her eyes. "According to a slab of sandstone dated 1834 and inscribed with a desperate message from a fellow named Ezra Kind, he and his six companions had mined gold in the area, his companions had all been killed by Indians, and the Indians were now after Kind. Apparently,

Kind didn't make it out alive, because a gold rush didn't occur in the Black Hills until the 1870s."

"In 1887," continued Joe, "a local resident named Louis Thoen . . ."

"Tell them what Thoen did for a living," said Gertie.

"He was a stone cutter," Joe answered reluctantly.

"How convenient," said Gertie.

"Anyway," continued Joe, "Thoen found Ezra Kind's inscribed slab near Spearfish, and it's now known as the Thoen Stone. If the Thoen Stone is authentic, and I happen to believe it is, it means the first discovery of gold in the West did not occur at Sutter's Mill in California in 1848 as widely believed, but rather right here in the Black Hills in the 1830s."

"What a brilliant story," said Maurice. "Gertie, something tells me you don't believe it."

"No I don't," answered Gertie. "I think old Thoen was a prankster. A man after my own heart."

"There's been extensive research on the subject," Joe said." Let me show you one of the books."

He got up from the table to scan the bookcase in the living room.

"Here it is. *The Thoen Stone* by Frank Thomson. Since I have a couple of copies, I'd like to give you this one," Joe said as he handed the book to Maurice. "It will make a believer out of you."

"You have both been so generous," Maurice said as he flipped through his gift. "I'll accept this book only if you two sign it." He handed the book to Gertie.

With a mischievous look on her face, Gertie got up from the table and removed a couple of items from a nearby desk. Out of Maurice's view, she attached an object to the title page of the book before writing a message and handing it to Joe, who smiled as he signed his name.

"It's just me," Gordon said as he politely knocked on the screen door before joining us.

I hadn't even realized Gordon had left. He handed four CDs to Maurice, who produced a pen from his jacket before writing a note on each sleeve.

"To thank you for this lovely afternoon," Maurice said as he presented the music to Gertie, "here are the Bee Gees' two latest CDs. There are copies for you and Joe and another set for Angela. Do you have a CD player?"

"We do in the car," said Joe.

"Good. The red CD is a greatest hits record. Gertie, you might recognize some of the songs on that one. Joe, I'm sorry, but we didn't cover any Gene Autry songs."

"That's all right," Joe said as he handed *The Thoen Stone* to Maurice. "I hope you enjoy this book as much as I do."

"I'm sure I will, Joe."

Maurice opened the front cover and read the inscription to himself before he let out a hearty laugh and read the message aloud.

To Maurice,

We thoroughly enjoyed meeting you and your friends today. Thank you for the memorable afternoon.

As a token of our appreciation, we hereby bestow upon you the title of honorary member of the city of Maurice (pronounced the correct way,) and thereby present you with a key to the city.

Your friends,
Gertie, Angela and Joe Sullivan
Maurice, South Dakota
May 19, 2002

Taped to the right of their message was an old skeleton key.

"I think the key used to unlock the original door to the cabin," said Gertie.

"Do you mind if I give your wife a hug?" Maurice asked Joe.

"Who cares what he thinks," said Gertie. "I'll take that hug. And one for Angela, too."

Chapter 19

"RIGHT NOW WE'RE at the northern edge of the Black Hills," said Nick as we passed a sign announcing the population of Spearfish at just under seven thousand.

"That's an unusual name," said Maurice.

"Spearfish got its name from the Indians in the area who would catch their fish . . ."

"By spearing them," added Maurice.

"I've tried spearing fish before," said Nick. "It's more difficult than you'd think."

"Spearfish is one of the few towns in the Hills that wasn't a mining settlement," I said. "It was a cow town, a farming and ranching community. Now it's an active college town. There's always something fun do in Spearfish."

"Mo," I added, "do you remember the people you met at Crazy Horse yesterday?"

"Why yes I do. There was Pauline and Nita from New Jersey and Jennifer and Peter from Belle Fourche."

"Impressive," I said.

"But not the least bit surprising," added Gordon, "coming from Mo."

"Well Jennifer and Peter live maybe ten, fifteen miles north of here," I said.

"Let's pop in and surprise them with a visit," said Maurice. "They did invite us after all."

"But we don't know their last name," said Gordon.

"And the population of Belle Fourche is around five thousand, so we'd probably have to knock on quite a few doors to find them."

"I suppose you're right," said Maurice. "Plus, the afternoon is going by quick enough."

AFTER DRIVING THROUGH Spearfish, we headed south on the interstate to complete the last leg of our loop of the Hills and to give Maurice a chance to see how the Mini Cooper performed at the legal speed limit of 75 miles an hour. Since there didn't appear to be highway patrol officers in the area, he even pushed the Mini a bit faster.

"Gordon. We're coming up on Sturgis," said Maurice. "Do you want to stop?"

"Of course," answered Gordon.

Maurice and Gordon were surprised at the ordinary appearance of the town.

"Fifty weeks out of the year Sturgis is a nice, quiet town of about five-thousand people," said Nick. "Then, in early August it's transformed into a city of a couple hundred thousand of the rowdiest people in the world."

Maurice parked the Mini Cooper next to a city sign and had me take a couple of pictures as proof of Gordon and Maurice's visit to Sturgis.

Nick then directed Maurice to drive a couple miles east of Sturgis.

"This is Fort Meade," Nick said as Maurice drove toward the entrance of a former frontier cavalry post.

"The fort was established, I think in 1878, to protect local settlers from Native Americans," continued Nick. "What was left of the Seventh Cavalry after the Battle of Little Bighorn was even posted there."

"This is a fantastic place," said Maurice as he drove us past the numerous original buildings that still exist on the grounds.

"What's it used for now?" asked Gordon.

"The large building we just passed is a Veterans Administration hospital," said Nick. "And I believe the South Dakota National Guard uses this as a training site."

"Nick," I said, "tell them about Fort Meade's connection to the 'Star Spangled Banner.'"

"I didn't know one existed," answered Nick.

"Really?" I said. "Well, sometime before the turn of the century and quite a while before it became our National Anthem, Fort Meade's commander called for the playing of the 'Star Spangled Banner' at the beginning of military ceremonies at the post. I believe his actions helped to make the song what it is today."

"From now on," said Maurice, "when I hear the 'Star Spangled Banner,' I will think of our visit to Fort Meade. And to that volcano-looking mountain. What is that?"

Maurice pointed to an impressive-looking peak located a few miles to the northeast of Fort Meade.

"That," I answered, "is Bear Butte. It's a state park now. But it's also a significant landmark for Native Americans in the area. They, and actually people from all around the world, make pilgrimages to Bear Butte for spiritual and healing purposes."

"If we had time," added Nick, "we'd take you and Gordon on the two-mile trail to the top."

"Next time," said Maurice.

"That and a trip to see Jennifer and Peter in Belle Fourche," added Gordon.

"I'll start working on the itinerary right away," I said.

"And you know she will," added Nick.

ONCE BACK ON the road Maurice said, "This may be our last chance to play Name that Car Tune. Do I have any takers?"

Nick and Gordon were busy talking about the Sturgis rally, so Maurice directed his next comment to me.

"You've proven to be such an admirable player, Caroline, that I propose to make the game a little tougher. Now, we also have to give the year the song was released and the name of the composer."

"You'll win for sure," I said. "How about the year *or* the composer."

"Fair enough," Maurice said as he turned the radio up and switched to the FM dial.

". . .escape from reality. . ."

"Queen. 'Bohemian Rhapsody,'" Maurice said. "Let's see, it came out in 1975 and was written by Mr. Mercury."

"How do I know you're not guessing," I said. "Are you sure it's not Mercury and May, or Mercury and Deacon or, who's the other one?"

"Taylor," answered Maurice.

"Right, how do you know it's not Mercury and Taylor."

"Because I know these things."

"Did Freddie write all their songs?" I asked.

"No, all four of them composed. But Freddie happened to write this one by himself. Just listen to their harmony. Weren't they fabulous?"

We sang along with Freddie and his band mates as Maurice sped up to pass a car.

"I saw that," said Maurice.

"What?" I said.

"You stopped singing because you didn't want the driver of the other car to know you were singing."

"I guess I did, didn't I."

"I used to do the same thing," confessed Maurice.

"You did?"

"Like most everyone else, until one day when I decided to do my part to break humankind of that odd habit."

". . .'cause I'm looking. . ."

"'Crawling in the Dark' by Hoobastank," said Maurice. "It came out this year and was written by Estrin and Robb.

"How the blank do you know that?" I asked.

"I like to keep up with new music, same as you," answered Maurice. "Plus, I take special interest in Hoobastank since a couple of its members are fans of ours."

"Bet that makes you feel good," I said.

"It absolutely does."

"What kind of music do you listen to?" I asked.

"All types really, except for rap," said Maurice. "I just can't get enthused about rap. But you'll never hear me put down those who do. I don't want to be like those people who thought rock'n'roll was the work of the devil. That was insane."

"That's right," I said. "You experienced the birth of rock first hand, didn't you? What was that like?"

"From what I can remember, because I was quite young at the time, it was unbelievably exciting and it was unstoppable. My God, can you believe it's been close to fifty years."

"Anyway," continued Maurice, "you Americans are familiar with Bill Haley and the Comets, who helped popularize rock'n'roll with 'Rock Around the Clock.' But at the same time, skiffle was all the rage in England."

"What's skiffle?" I asked.

"It's a combination of blues and folk and jazz. It originated years earlier, I believe in rural America, and with ordinary household items like washboards and jugs and with homemade guitars and banjos. But Lonnie Donegan made it popular in England by emphasizing its raw elements, which appealed to England's budding musicians, like Tommy Steele. Made them feel like they could make their own music."

"Tommy who?" I asked.

"Tommy Steele. England's version of Elvis." Maurice added with a chuckle, "Barry used to pretend days on end he was Tommy."

"Not much later, rock crossed the pond," continued Maurice. "So, then England had both rock and skiffle. Although skiffle was, and still is popular, in fact, Lonnie's still touring, rock became the more dominant of the two. Anyhow, these new sounds were so different from anything we'd ever heard before. It literally caused a revolution. Kids went crazy over this upbeat, energetic music. Their parents, on the other hand, were not so thrilled."

"How'd your parents react?" I asked.

"Fortunately, or unfortunately," answered Maurice, "they liked it. Our friends, in an attempt to show their independence, would boast about how their mums and dads despised the music. We couldn't join in because our parents rather enjoyed it."

"Have you ever met Lonnie or Tommy?" I asked.

"Better yet," said Maurice, "we've worked with both of them. Tommy even recorded one of our songs."

"How about Elvis? Did you ever meet him?"

"I did, around the time he recorded 'Words.' I was so star struck then, after all he was the King. And he was wonderful. I can't say enough good things about the man."

"Elvis performed in Rapid City," said Nick. "I went to the concert."

"Nick, I didn't know you saw Elvis," I said as I turned toward him. "I went to the concert in Sioux Falls the night after the Rapid concert."

"Elvis performed in South Dakota the summer of '77," I said to Maurice, "in fact, just a few months before he died. He opened the new civic center in Rapid and then performed in Sioux Falls and a few other Midwestern venues."

"How was the concert?" asked Maurice.

"I didn't realize how good of a singer Elvis was until I saw him live," said Nick.

"That's exactly how I felt," I added. "His voice was fabulous, and this was at the point when the critics said his talent was fading."

"Speaking of Rapid City," I continued, "here we are. The biggest city between Sioux Falls and Denver."

"Except for Sturgis in August," added Gordon.

"Rapid's a nice town," I said. "Its population is around sixty thousand and, if you include the surrounding areas, there's maybe a hundred thousand. Big enough for me."

I navigated Maurice through a leisurely tour of the city, which concluded with an impressive spin on Skyline Drive.

When we arrived on Rapid's southwestern edge, Nick pointed to the Black Hills in the distance. "Gordon, Mo, do you see that peak over there? The highest one?"

"You're not going to tell us that's Harney Peak way up there, are you?" asked Maurice. Before Nick could reply, Maurice added, "You mean we actually hiked all the way up there? I'm surprised my whole body isn't sore."

WE ARRIVED IN our driveway just before the sun set. Nick and I went around the back of the house to let Shelby out of her kennel while Maurice and Gordon stayed near the vehicles to talk. Nick and I assumed Maurice and Gordon were having a private conversation, so we walked Shelby on the far side of the house.

After a respectable amount of time, we brought Shelby around to the front of the house so she could perform her duty as official greeter. When she spotted Maurice, she ambled toward him with her wiggle butt.

"What a good girl. Shelby, shake."

Shelby swiftly lifted her left paw. Maurice shook it for a few seconds and then bent down to kiss her on the head.

"Thank you sweetie," said Maurice. "Now do me a favor. Go to Gordon and shake hands with him."

Shelby obediently strutted over to Gordon, sat in front of him, and raised her left paw. Gordon laughed before shaking Shelby's paw.

"If that doesn't turn you into a dog lover," said Maurice, "I don't know what will."

"Okay, I concede," said Gordon. "She's a great dog. She's even smarter than a lot of people I know. But I wouldn't go so far as to say I'm a dog lover, more of a dog liker." "You are a good girl though, aren't you, Shelby," Gordon said as bent down to scratch her behind both ears.

"I heard that Gordon," said Maurice. "I knew you had a dog voice."

"What are you talking about?"

"You know," answered Maurice. "The voice people use when they talk to dogs. This weekend has been a success. Gordon has found his dog voice."

"I better leave before you have any plans for me finding my cat voice," said Gordon.

Chapter 20

MAURICE, NICK, AND I were still wound up from the day's activities. We decided to relax on the front porch and watch the remnants of daylight melt into the Hills. Shelby lay down on one side of Maurice's chair and Tom Cat settled down in his lap.

"What a weekend," Maurice said as he scratched Tom behind his ears. "How did we manage to fit so much into so little time?"

"And we didn't even touch the tip of the iceberg," I said. "We didn't get to Devil's Tower, Wounded Knee, the Badlands, the Rochford area, Needles Highway, some old Civilian Conservation Corps camps . . ."

"The Thoen Stone," added Maurice.

"Who could forget the Thoen Stone," I said.

"Apparently you, and I'll never forgive you for that," Maurice said with a wink.

"Mo, you might have enjoyed The Mammoth Site in Hot Springs," said Nick. "It's a working paleontological museum."

"Here in South Dakota?" asked Maurice.

"The state is full of surprises," I answered.

"I'm beginning to find that out," said Maurice. "So, what's with this museum?"

"Well in the 1970s," said Nick, "a construction company unearthed some skeletal remains. When one of the workers brought a bone home, his young son, who had just been studying fossils in school, persuaded his dad to let him find out if the bone was a fossil. Come to find out, it belonged to a mammoth that had fallen into a sinkhole some twenty-five thousand years earlier. So far, the remains of that mammoth and fifty of his buddies have been excavated from the site."

"Speaking of fossils," I said, "have you heard of the Tyrannosaurus Rex named Sue?"

Answering with a respectable Johnny Cash impersonation, Maurice said, "No, but I've heard of a boy named Sue."

"The sex of the dinosaur's a mystery," I said, "so I guess it could be a boy named Sue. Anyway, Sue, which is the largest T-Rex ever found, was discovered in the Badlands."

"Why the unusual name?" asked Maurice. "Sure, Sue's a nice name, but not one I'd consider for a dinosaur."

"Sue was named after the paleontologist who found her," answered Nick.

"Caroline, we should have taken Mo and Gordon spelunking," said Nick.

"Can you do that in mixed company?" asked Maurice.

"Only in dark, tight spaces," Nick answered with a straight face before adding, "Spelunking's a fancy name for cave exploring. There are a number of caves along the perimeter of the Hills. Most tourists take the typical guided tour. You know, with guard rails and lights on the walls. But on a spelunking tour, your only aid is the light on your hat."

"Like a miner's hat," said Maurice.

"Exactly, I added. "And we look a lot like miners when we emerge from the cave because of the tight crevices we have to maneuver through. You wouldn't believe how filthy we get. But that's half the fun."

"So it's good clean, filthy fun," said Maurice. "Don't you two ever relax on weekends?"

"No, we relax when we're at work," I said.

THE EVENING AIR was turning chilly, so four of us moved into the house, while the fifth chased after a chipmunk that had wandered onto the porch. Nick built a fire to ward off the coolness that had crept into the house. I turned on the TV and handed the remote to Maurice who watched a news network for a couple of minutes before switching to a music channel.

"You like music videos?" I asked.

"I watch too many for my own good," said Maurice.

"Believe it or not," I said, "I've never really gotten into music videos, so pardon my ignorance. But have the Bee Gees made many?"

"We made videos years before MTV even existed," said Maurice. "But our first official music video for the MTV era was for 'You Win Again' back in 1987. That was off the first album we'd released since the early 80s."

"How did *ESP* do?" I asked.

Maurice smiled when I mentioned the name of the album.

"It went all the way to number one in England and a few other countries overseas, and it made it into the top hundred in America. So we were very pleased. Our next record . . ."

"*One*," I added.

"Yes, did even better in America."

Maurice paused briefly before continuing. "*One* was a bittersweet album though, since Andy had died the year before. He would have been so thrilled that America was warming back to us."

Shelby sat down next to Maurice and put her head on his knee.

"Yes, Andy would have liked that, wouldn't he have Shelby," Maurice said as he stroked her head.

"Where do you go to record, Mo?" asked Nick. "New York?"

"We have before, yes. Now we usually record in our Miami studio."

"Isn't that like giving free reign to a child in a candy store?" I asked.

"You know me very well, don't you, Caroline," replied Maurice. "I've always loved tinkering with the studio equipment. And despite that, some of it still works."

"So you enjoy the recording process?" I asked.

"I absolutely love it."

"Have you released all of the songs you've recorded?" I asked.

"Far from it. I've personally laid down hundreds of songs on demo tapes that haven't seen the light of day."

"Why not?"

"Some didn't fit in with the record we were making at the time. Others are unfinished. And, to be honest, a few are absolutely dreadful. But that's all and well. As long as I keep working at my craft every day, I'll be a happy man."

"You don't do it just for the money?" asked Nick.

"I'd be lying if I said money didn't matter, but it rarely motivates me."

"I bet I can name one of those times when it did," said Nick. "Didn't you put out an album that raised a nice amount of money for charity?"

"You must be referring to *Music for UNICEF*," answered Maurice.

"Yes, I am," said Nick. "I bought the album and I think I still have it. I'll be right back."

Nick sprinted toward the bedroom. A few minutes later, he came back waving his *Music for UNICEF Concert* album in the air.

"I almost forgot about this," said Nick. "I bought it because Olivia Newton-John had a couple of songs on it. She was hot. Well, of course, I also bought it because of the Bee Gees."

"I believe you Nick," said Maurice.

160

"No, I actually was a Bee Gees fan back then, er, still am a Bee Gees fan," said Nick.

"Apparently a closet Bee Gees fan," said Maurice.

"Apparently so," I said. "I never knew you had this album, Nick. Can I see it?"

Nick held the record out to me and then yanked it away just before I could grab it. He quickly relinquished it after I threatened to draw a mustache on Olivia Newton-John's face.

"The three of us," said Maurice, "along with Robert Stigwood, conceived the idea for the concert and the album, with all the proceeds going to UNICEF. We had no problem recruiting artists. They were all so eager to participate."

I read off the names listed on the album cover. "Earth, Wind, and Fire; Andy; Donna Summer; a duet with Andy and Olivia Newton-John; ABBA; Rod Stewart; Olivia by herself; John Denver; Kris Kristofferson and Rita Coolidge; and, of course, the Bee Gees. This belongs in a 1970s-time capsule."

"How much money did the album raise?" Nick asked.

"Well over ten million dollars initially. And it's still raising money. The Bee Gees' contribution to the album was 'Too Much Heaven.' Since 'Heaven' is on our new greatest hits CD, some of those profits will go to UNICEF."

"Even though the song was released more than twenty years ago?" asked Nick.

"Even though," said Maurice.

"I know how you'll answer this," said Nick. "But did you consider not including 'Too Much Heaven' on the new CD so you could keep more of the profits?"

"Now why hadn't I thought of that," said Maurice. "But seriously, we're thrilled 'Heaven' is still raising money. At the time we announced its royalties would go to UNICEF, we had no idea how popular 'Heaven' would be because we hadn't even released it yet. As it turned out, it went to number one in America."

"Are you good at predicting which of your songs will be hits?" I asked.

"Not necessarily. Sometimes, songs we think will be popular go nowhere, while others we hadn't planned on releasing as singles end up with big followings."

I was about to ask Maurice what songs he was referring to when Nick said, "Since I got away with a cynical question earlier, I'll take my chances with another one. Aren't you essentially required to do charity work if you're famous?"

"That's a fair question. Cynical yes, but fair nonetheless," said Maurice. "You hope the main reason you perform charity work is for the sake of those you're helping. Plus, there's no way I'll be able to sensibly spend all the money I've earned. So it only makes sense to help others if you can. But in the back of your mind, you're also aware that your public charity work won't hurt your image. And unfortunately, in this business image is everything."

"Do you ever give anonymous donations?" asked Nick.

"It wouldn't be anonymous if I told you now, would it?" said Maurice.

Shelby started to bark at a pair of headlights in the driveway. Nick and I sprinted to the window to see if we recognized the vehicle.

"I'm not expecting anyone. Are you, Nick?"

"No," he answered as he collected his jacket. "I'll go see who it is. C'mon Shelby Lee."

From inside, Maurice and I could hear Shelby barking at the vehicle, which had stopped in the driveway.

"You don't need an expensive security system," said Maurice. "You have Shelby."

"Yes," I answered, "but if a burglar were to offer her a dog biscuit, she'd gladly hold his flashlight and lead him to our fine china."

After the car turned around, Shelby and Nick came back in the house.

"Who was it?" I asked.

"A teenage couple who thought this was lover's lane. I think Shelby sounded ferocious enough to discourage them from coming back."

"I have to admit," said Maurice, "that my vain side thought they might be friends you'd invited over to meet me."

Nick and I grinned at each other.

"We had seriously considered throwing a small party tonight in your honor," Nick said.

"You know me well enough now to realize I would have appreciated the party," said Maurice. "But I'm actually relieved you didn't plan a get-together. I'm enjoying myself tonight, just relaxing with the three of you."

"Quick, Nick," I shouted. "Call everyone. Tell 'em the party's off."

Before Maurice could react, I added, "Just kidding, Mo. Actually, Nick's the one who wanted to throw the party. But I reminded him we didn't know what time we'd get home tonight."

"That's not the real reason, though, is it Caroline?" said Nick.

"Sure it is," I answered.

"No, it's not. The real reason is you didn't want to share Mo with a lot of other people," said Nick.

I felt my face blush. "Well, if you knew, why didn't you let on earlier?"

"Because I didn't want to embarrass you," answered Nick.

"No, you'd rather wait until Mo was here, so you could watch me turn beet red in front of him,"

"I'm sorry Caroline. I didn't mean to get you flustered," replied Nick before he turned to Maurice and added, "I just got lucky it turned out that way."

"You do know, Nicholas," I said, "that paybacks are hell."

"Promises, promises. I'm actually more worried about how our friends will react once they realize we didn't invite them to meet Mo."

"Do we have to tell them?" I said.

"Right. I've never known you to keep a secret," said Nick.

"No really. This can be our little, I mean, big secret. Let's at least try."

"I'm actually impressed you've kept Mo a secret for this long," said Nick. "But why don't you want to tell anyone?"

"It's hard to explain," I said. "But when you let others in on something special, it's not just yours anymore. And then it tends to lose its significance. If we told people about Mo and Gordon's visit, this weekend wouldn't belong to us anymore."

"Caroline, if you feel so strongly about it," said Nick, "I'll go along with your wishes. But, if you happen to tell anyone, you have to . . ."

He attempted to whisper the remainder in my ear.

Before he could finish, I pushed him away and said, "You wish."

Maurice chuckled as he picked up my acoustic guitar from its stand next to the piano.

"That hasn't been played for half a year, Mo," I said. "No doubt it's seriously out of tune."

Maurice slid the strap over his right shoulder, strummed a few chords, and said, "It doesn't sound half bad," which he followed up with a comical frown.

"Which also means," I added, "it doesn't sound half good."

"You stole my line," laughed Maurice.

After spending a moment tuning the guitar, Maurice said, "There, that's more like it."

Catching us by surprise, he began playing one of the most famous riffs known to man. Immediately recognizing the opening notes of "Stayin' Alive," Nick and I leapt from our seats and attempted to strut our stuff like John Travolta. Despite our feeble efforts, Maurice continued to play as he lent his vocals to the first verse. Nick and I eagerly joined in on the chorus.

"I'm impressed, Mo," I said as Maurice plucked the final notes of the song. "I thought you could only play that on a bass guitar."

"You mean this isn't a bass?" said Maurice.

"You could probably make 'Stayin' Alive' sound good on a ukulele," said Nick.

Eager to take on a challenge, Maurice managed to make the guitar sound like a ukulele as he repeated the introduction.

"So, do you know any other songs, Mr. Guitar Extraordinaire?" I asked.

"A few. Let's see if you can name this tune," he said as he began playing an energetic, funky melody.

I replied using our car tune format, "'This is Where I Came In.' The Bee Gees. 2001. Written by Barry, Robin, and Maurice Gibb."

I finished just before Maurice began to sing. He acknowledged my professionalism by nodding. Finally, my year at the radio station paid off as I was able to uphold the deejays' first cardinal rule—no talking over the lyrics.

As Maurice continued, Nick performed a low-key version of the white-man's overbite while I played air drums and sang backup vocals.

Maurice caught my eye when we neared the close of the song and made a "slash" gesture to indicate we'd finish with a cold ending rather than a fade.

". . . I came in."

"Caroline you make a marvelous backup-singer," Maurice said as he lifted the guitar strap from around his head. "A few times there I wanted to yell, 'Back up, back up!'"

"My life is now complete," I replied with a smile. "I've been ribbed by Mo Gibb."

"Let's see how you do on keyboards, my dear," Maurice said as he sat down at the piano and patted the bench space to his left. "I want to teach you an extremely simple tune, which you will then play as you accompany me on this next song."

Although I was reluctant to show off my rusty piano skills, I eagerly sat next to him. With his left hand, he played eight bars of a very simple, but catchy tune.

After repeating it, Maurice said, "I know it's complicated, but I think you can pull it off. Let's have a go."

I got it right on the second try.

"Brilliant," said Maurice. "Now I want you to play this movement throughout the song."

"Piece of cake," I replied.

"Oh, by the way," added Maurice nonchalantly, "Did I tell you about the key changes?"

"No," I whined, "Not dreaded key changes."

"You'll do fine," he countered. Then he played the passage in two different keys. I repeated it back to him, cringing when I hit a few wrong notes.

"Tell you what. I'll take Shelby outside so she can do her business and so I can have a smoke. You can practice while we're out."

I was so busy concentrating that I barely noticed when Maurice and Nick put on their jackets and led Shelby out the main door. By the time they came back in the house, I was able to play the song without any mistakes.

"Two more small additions I need to show you," said Maurice. "There's a two-bar introduction that goes like this . . . You'll play it a couple of times during the song. I'll cue you when. Plus, toward the end of the song, when the tempo slows, I want you to play the notes as running chords. Like this," he said as he demonstrated.

I repeated the new segments a few times before I said, "Got it."

"Oh, I forgot to tell you the most important part," said Maurice as he placed his right hand on my left shoulder. "Have fun."

He slid the guitar strap back over his head and said, "You ready?"

"Ready."

"I'll give you a count of four," said Maurice.

"Give me a couple," I answered. I had butterflies in my stomach.

"I'll give you as many as you need. Just jump in when you're ready. One-two-three-four-and-one-two-three-four-and . . ."

On the next beat, I started playing the quaint, spirited "Spicks and Specks." Maurice began singing on the third bar and added guitar at the third verse.

To my amazement, I played the first half with near perfection. Midway, Maurice cued me for the first key change, which I transitioned into smoothly. Eight bars later, I changed keys again. And after another eight bars, he cued me for the chord pattern. At this point, he slowed down the tempo by drawing out the notes he sang and strummed. When we neared the end of this verse, Maurice cued me to play the introduction again, which I performed with such gusto that it elicited a gorgeous smile from Maurice.

"I've found my new keyboardist," Maurice said as we finished the song. "Your piano teacher would be proud."

"Proud and perhaps a bit offended," I said. "He could never motivate me like you just did, Mo. You're a wonderful teacher. Nick, did that sound as good as I thought it did?"

"It sounded like you two have been performing together for years."

"Can you teach me one more song?" I said.

"Sure. And since you've proven yourself on 'Spicks and Specks,' I'll teach you both the right and left hands on this next song."

That's right, I thought to myself, I had just played the left hand on "Spicks and Specks." What had I gotten myself into?

"I need to warn you, Mo. It takes me a while to get both hands down."

"Don't cut yourself short. You play better than you think," Maurice said as he sat down next to me.

Despite my reservations, he taught me how to play a simplified version of "Alone" within a matter of minutes. After I shooed the three of them back outside, it struck me how much I was enjoying my practice session. Who'd a thought.

Cold air snuck in behind the trio when they came back in the house a few minutes later.

"I promise I won't send you outside anymore tonight," I said.

"Good," said Nick. "Because we wouldn't have gone."

"Are you ready to wow them again, Caroline?" Maurice said as he picked up the guitar

"You bet," I announced.

"Since we both begin at the same time on this number, I'll let you give the count," said Maurice.

"Okay. Ready?"

"Ready."

"One-two-three-four-and-," I counted.

On the next beat Maurice and I began "Alone" together. I felt fairly comfortable with the piano arrangement, so I lent my vocals to the song, particularly on the echo parts in the chorus.

When we neared the end, Maurice said, "Finish with a glissando."

He demonstrated by gliding his right hand through the air. As he played "Alone's" last notes on the guitar, I slid my right-hand fingers across the white keys and then flamboyantly raised them in the air to punctuate the end of the song.

"Brilliant," said Maurice as he and Nick cheered. Shelby joined in the accolade by lifting her nose and proclaiming, "Woo, woo, woo."

"I can't tell you how good that felt," I said as I got up from the piano. "Mo, you sure have an infectious way with music. I never in my wildest dreams imagined I'd play piano well enough to accompany anyone, let alone you."

"That's quite a compliment," said Maurice demurely as he returned the guitar to its stand.

I almost suggested we break out a bottle of wine before I caught myself.

Shelby, who had retrieved a brush from her basket, waited for me to take it from her mouth.

"If you don't mind," said Maurice, "I'd like to comb Shelby tonight."

At the mention of her name, she trotted over to Maurice, presented him with the brush, and lay down on the rug in front of him.

"You *are* a dog lover, Mo," I said.

"I didn't tell you, but another reason I took your invitation seriously was your mention of owning a Golden Retriever. Anyone who has a Golden must have character."

"Oh we're a couple of characters, all right," I said.

"Yes, I've come to realize that," said Maurice.

After he was satisfied with his work on Shelby's left side, Maurice caught my eye and said, "Shelby, other side."

Obediently, Shelby stood up, turned around, and lay down on her left side.

"Good girl," proclaimed Maurice. "Good girl."

Chapter 21

MY ALARM WENT off at five o'clock Monday morning. I lay in bed for a few minutes thinking about how different the house would be once Maurice left. For a moment, I wished he hadn't come so I wouldn't have to say goodbye to him. I quickly berated myself for thinking such a thought and spent the next few minutes reflecting on the extraordinary weekend. Eager to begin the day after the attitude adjustment, I got out of bed, showered, tried to make myself look beautiful, and then put on a pot of coffee.

"Good morning, Caroline," Maurice said as he and Shelby glided down the stairs a few minutes later.

"Good morning, Mo. You're up early," I said as Shelby rushed to my side.

"I didn't want to miss any second of this morning," he said as he gave me a friendly hug and a kiss on the cheek.

Maurice and I laughed and pointed at each other when we noticed both of us were wearing our Harney Peak t-shirts.

"Do you normally wake up so early, Mo?"

"No, I love to sleep in." He glanced at his watch. "At home, I'd be getting up about this time, what with the two-hour time difference, which reminds me. I owe Nick an apology."

"Why's that?"

"Since Shelby kept me company last night, he couldn't go jogging with her this morning."

"He should thank you. It gave him a good reason to sleep in," I said. "The coffee's almost ready. Or can I make you some tea? I forgot about the Brits' fondness for hot tea until Gertie offered you some yesterday."

"Not all Brits drink tea," said Maurice.

"Do you?"

"Yes," answered Maurice. "And not all South Dakotans drive pickups. Do you?"

"Yes," I replied.

We grinned at each other.

"Coffee sounds good this morning," said Maurice. "While it's brewing I hope you don't mind me taking Shelby out."

"So you can both use the outdoor facilities?" I said.

"Perhaps," he said as he collected his jacket.

While they were gone, I finished cutting up some of the fruit Maurice has given us on Friday and took the cinnamon-walnut muffins out of the oven. Maurice knocked on the front door before he and Shelby bounded back in the house.

"Something smells fabulous," he said as he placed the morning paper on a chair. "I hope you didn't go to a lot of bother."

"Like I grudgingly agreed to last night, I made a fairly simple breakfast."

Maurice poured himself a cup of coffee while I filled Shelby's dog dish and water bowl.

After finishing her breakfast, she raced over to me for her morning pills.

"Now there's something, a dog who likes medicine," said Maurice.

"I assume the pills taste good. Either that or she realizes the pills make her feel better," I said as I joined Maurice at the table.

Shelby gently plopped down under the table and placed her head on my left foot.

"Have you always had dogs?" asked Maurice.

"Surprisingly no. I used to consider myself strictly a cat person. I've always owned cats."

"I love cats, too."

"I figured that," I said. "I'll bet you even love grouchy cats."

"Of course. Grouchy cats need just as much loving as affectionate ones do."

I smiled at the thought of Maurice picking up an ill-tempered cat and turning it into a purring feline within a matter of seconds.

"I agree and I've had my share of grouchy cats. Anyway, Shelby is the first dog I've ever really owned."

"I find that hard to believe. The two of you get along so well that I assumed you've had a pack of other dogs."

"Well, Nick has always owned dogs," I said. "He had an older German shepherd, named Beauty, when we got married. I was leery about having a dog as a pet probably because I had a dog phobia when I was young."

"I can't see you being afraid of dogs," said Maurice.

"I was though. I used to be terrified of dogs. So it was a relief and a nice surprise when I got along well with Beauty."

"All it takes is one good dog to turn things around," said Maurice.

"You're right. And Beauty was that dog. When she passed away, I grieved for her as much as Nick did. So when he brought up the idea of getting another dog, I enthusiastically agreed."

"We settled on a Golden Retriever," I added, "probably because Nick had never owned one and wanted to try a different type of dog and we had heard so many good things about the breed."

"Goldens are more than pets," said Maurice. "They're family."

"They really are," I agreed. "Years from now I know I'll still consider Shelby as a member of our family."

"I hate to admit it," I added, "but this last year Shelby's been aging quickly. I'm hoping the pills I give her will slow down the deterioration in her joints."

"It's hard seeing a pet grow old, isn't it," Maurice said. "Particularly when they've been such an important part of your life."

"It's real hard," I replied, trying to mask the lump that was growing in my throat. "When the time comes, I know I won't handle it very well."

"Perhaps you can take comfort in knowing that a part of her will always be with you," said Maurice.

I leaned forward to scratch Shelby under her left ear. "Quoting your lyrics from 'The Lord,' I hope her soul sticks around. At least for a while."

SHELBY SCRAMBLED TOWARD Nick when he emerged from the bedroom.

"Morning, Shelby," Nick said as he crouched down to pet her. "I only wish my wife would greet me the same way you do. Yes I do, don't I, Shelby."

"But Nick," I said as I got up from the table, "I didn't think you liked me licking your face."

I gave him a dry kiss on my way to the kitchen. Nick poured himself a cup of coffee and sat down next to Maurice. While they exchanged good mornings, I put the fruit, muffins, cereal, and milk on the table.

"Wouldn't it be nice to have a leisurely breakfast like this every morning," I said to Nick as we began eating. "I think I'll go in at noon every day from now on."

"Only if I can too," said Nick.

After breakfast we refilled our coffee cups and assumed our familiar seats in the screened-in porch to watch the big-horn sheep feast on the lawn and to listen to the birds sing their morning songs. Tom came in through the porch's cat access and began crunching on his dried food, which somewhat muffled the birds' tunes.

Shelby and Maurice jumped up simultaneously when they heard the Range Rover approach.

"I'll go bring Gordon around. You two stay here," Maurice said as he sprinted out the porch door.

A few minutes later, Maurice and Gordon made a commotion in the house before joining us on the porch. We exchanged pleasantries with Gordon before I went inside to pour a cup of coffee for him. While I had the opportunity, I glanced around the main floor to try to determine the source of Maurice and Gordon's clamor, but I didn't find anything out of the ordinary.

"How was your stay at the B&B, Gordo?" asked Maurice.

"It was great," answered Gordon. "But I can't say the same for some poor fellow at breakfast. There were about half a dozen of us at the same table. Three couples besides me. The women got on the subject of how their husbands proposed to them. One of the women, a newlywed I assume, was bragging about how her husband proposed to her at Niagara Falls. She said he even got down on one knee when he asked her to marry him."

Gordon chuckled before he continued. "But then her husband chimes in, 'No dear, you've got it all wrong. I tripped and asked if you would carry me.'"

Maurice and Nick laughed.

"That's what I thought," said Gordon, "But his wife didn't see the humor in it. She was so upset she poured a glass of orange juice over his head and stormed out of the room."

"Quite a sticky situation, eh," said Maurice, "Nick, orange you glad Caroline can take a joke?"

I tried unsuccessfully to stifle a grin.

"How about you, Mo?" asked Nick. "Seems like your wife would need an especially good sense of humor to keep up with you."

"She married me didn't she?" replied Maurice.

"You do know you could make a living as a stand-up comedian," I said.

"I actually tried it once, but the audience told me to sit down," replied Maurice. "But seriously, if you think I'm funny you should meet Robin."

"Rob can be extremely shy around people he's just met," continued Maurice. "So unfortunately Caroline, he probably didn't show off his full personality to you on the phone yesterday. However, to those who know him well, he is hands down the funniest person ever. If I find myself in a lousy mood all I have to do is give Robin a ring and, within seconds, he'll have me laughing hysterically."

Maurice chuckled.

"I don't know how he does it, but all I have to do is think about Robin and he makes me laugh."

"I envy you for your brothers," I said. "Being an only child, I have no idea what it's like to joke around with siblings."

"Robin and Barry and I share a lot of laughs," said Maurice. "But we've also had our share of nasty quarrels. We're no different than any other family. We're actually quite ordinary."

"Right Mo," I said. "I've come to realize you're anything but ordinary."

Something outside prompted Shelby to scamper to the porch door and whine. When I opened the door, she dashed to the wood pile where a squirrel at the top taunted her with squeaks. At Maurice's suggestion, we followed her outside.

"Where does the trail lead?" Maurice asked, referring to the gravel road that extended past our driveway.

"It's a forest service road," answered Nick. "It leads to parts of the Hills that most people don't even know exist.

Too bad we didn't have time to take you and Gordon on the trail."

"How about right now?" asked Maurice. "Gordo, how we doing for time?"

Gordon glanced at his watch. "We're in luck. We can fit in a short walk."

The forest service trail was a lightly graveled road just wide enough to accommodate one vehicle. We followed the road as it curved to the left just beyond our house. Shelby ran past us to root out a turkey that had taken refuge in a shrub, while Tom trotted behind us. Nick shared his knowledge of the flora and fauna in the area as we followed the road up and down a series of small hills.

"I never get tired of coming back here," I said. "This is our little piece of heaven."

"I can see why you like it so much," said Maurice.

We reluctantly headed back after Gordon checked his watch.

When we reached the edge of our property, Maurice said, "Oh, I almost forgot." He ran in the house and came back carrying his camcorder. "I haven't shot any footage of your house."

Maurice instructed Nick, Shelby, and me—holding Tom Cat—to pose next to the house. Gordon joined us when we waved him into the picture. However, he politely declined my offer to hold Tom. After we hammed it up for the camera, Maurice walked around the yard shooting more footage.

"Make sure you get the outhouse," said Gordon.

Then Maurice herded us in our house to shoot the interior. When he finished, Gordon caught his eye and pointed toward his watch.

Maurice made a grimace before saying, "Well, I'd better gather up my things."

"I'll help," Nick said as he followed Maurice up the stairs.

They came back down carrying Maurice's belongings, which had more than tripled in size since Friday.

After depositing them near the front door, Maurice moved toward the sofa. "Caroline. Nick. Gordon and I want to give you a few gifts to show how much we enjoyed this weekend."

He picked up a tackle box he had hidden on the side of the sofa and handed it to Nick.

"This is great, guys," exclaimed Nick as he held up expensive-looking fishing gear. "Thank you. I can't wait to try it out."

Gordon then handed Nick a large bag that yielded a twenty-four pack of toilet paper.

"For the outhouse," said Gordon.

"And if I can keep Caroline's hands off of it," said Nick, "the pack should last me a good three years."

"Bet you'll never guess where I bought this," Maurice said handing me a jewelry box.

"At Mount Rushmore," I said as I lifted out a beautiful Black Hills Gold necklace. "I even helped you pick this out, but I had no idea it was for me. Thank you, Mo, Gordon."

Next he produced a small pouch of cat treats and a large rawhide bone, the latter which caught Shelby's attention.

"Do you think this is for you?" Maurice said as Shelby sat in front of him attentively.

"Woo," answered Shelby.

She gently took her present from Maurice's outstretched hands and retreated to the kitchen floor.

"If you can believe it," said Maurice, "Gordo even picked out these kitty treats for Tom Cat."

"I'm sure he'll appreciate them," I said.

Maurice and Gordon then slid out a large, flat object from underneath the sofa and carried it to the table.

"Caroline, this is for you," said Maurice, "although Nick may enjoy it as well."

Maurice anticipated the confused look on my face as I unwrapped a framed "Trafalgar."

"This isn't the print you gave me Friday," said Maurice. "I'm taking that home with me." He pointed to the long cylindrical container next to his bags.

"We, actually Gordon, found this framed version over the weekend."

The print was matted and framed in various shades of blue that blended nicely with the picture's dark blue and white image.

I was uncharacteristically speechless.

"Well, do you like it?" asked Maurice.

"It's gorgeous, Mo, I love it. You know you didn't have to do this, but thank you so much. And you too, Gordon." I attempted to pick up the picture. "I'm going to hang it over the piano."

Nick helped me hold the picture up to the wall above the keyboard.

"How does it look?" I asked.

"Perfect," said Maurice. "Absolutely perfect."

"One more present for you, Caroline," Maurice said. He handed me a CD and held onto an identical one.

The CD was titled *The Other Side of Shelby* and was credited to Maurice and me. The front cover included a picture of the two of us at Mount Rushmore. I read off the names of the songs listed on the back.

"'The Other Side of Shelby,' 'How Deep is Your Love,' 'Lonely Days,' 'Suddenly,' 'Trafalgar.' Mo, how'd you do this?"

"Remember when I played 'The Other Side of Shelby' on the keyboards Friday night? I recorded it because I didn't want to forget the melody. Well, I didn't realize until later that night when I played back the tape that I had forgotten to shut off the recorder after Shelby's song. Everything sounded so good on the tape that I thought you'd like a copy, thanks again to Gordon's legwork."

"This is priceless," I said.

"You don't know how right you are," Maurice said as he held up his copy. "We own the only two CDs pressed from the tape."

"That is unless someone's already made bootleg copies," Gordon added with a wicked grin.

"Will you sign my CD, Caroline?" asked Maurice.

"Only if you sign mine," I replied.

"I can't wait to listen to this," I said as we exchanged our inscribed CDs.

Maurice then nodded to Gordon, who picked up a handful of Maurice's bags and walked out the front door. Maurice and Nick followed with the remaining items while Shelby and I trailed behind.

After everything was loaded in the Range Rover, Maurice stood akimbo. "Gordo, do you want to drive the Mini to the airport?"

"Not particularly, no."

"There's a problem then, because I don't want to either. I guess we'll just have to leave it here."

"Guess so," agreed Gordon.

Maurice fished the Mini Cooper keys out of his pocket and tossed them to me.

"Hope you don't mind, Caroline," said Maurice, "but we rented the Mini until the end of the summer. It's yours and Nick's until then."

"We might find the time to drive it once or twice just to keep it in working order," I said with a bad poker face.

Maurice gave me a few pointers on the Mini while Gordon and Nick shot the breeze. They ended their banter by shaking hands and punching shoulders.

Gordon then walked over to Shelby who held out her left paw to him.

"You're a great dog," Gordon said as he shook her paw.

"Thanks to Shelby," he said to me as I wandered toward them, "I'm thinking of getting a dog."

"Oh I hope you do," I said. "You'd be great with a dog, Gordon."

"Gordo to you," he replied.

"Gordo," I repeated. "Thank you for everything you did for us this weekend."

"It was my pleasure. And thank you for the beautiful star quilt."

"It'll keep you warm if you ever get caught in a snow storm," I smiled.

Gordon smiled back before he added in a serious tone, "I enjoyed getting to know you and Nick these past few days. And you helped me more than you'll ever know. It was a great weekend."

"It really was," I agreed. "If you ever come back to the Hills, you are more than welcome to stay with us. At the very least, please look us up."

"I might just do that. I'm thinking of coming to Sturgis one of these years for the rally. Maybe even this summer. If I do, I promise I'll call you."

"You can even drive the Mini while you're here," I said. "In the meantime, I'll be on the lookout for Little House on the Prairie memorabilia for you."

"Then I'll have to come back," laughed Gordon.

We shared a heartfelt hug.

I then watched Gordon reluctantly take his place behind the wheel of the Range Rover.

I started to approach Maurice and Nick who were sharing a joke, but decided to give them some space.

Their conversation ended with a hug and pats on the back. Nick looked my way. "I think I'll leave you two alone."

He walked to the front door and waved to Maurice and Gordon before stepping inside.

"Caroline," said Maurice, "I don't have to tell you how marvelous this weekend has been."

"I was afraid you'd find us boring," I said trying to stay composed.

"Just the opposite. You have an exciting, refreshing life."

"You and your family are invited back here anytime."

"Don't be surprised if I take you up on your offer. But next time, I promise I'll give you more than a two-day notice."

Maurice glanced over at Shelby who was holding a pinecone in her mouth. When she caught him looking her way, she ambled over to him with her wiggle-butt.

"Shelby, you have a gift for me? I'm honored."

She sat in front of him and extended her left paw. Maurice knelt down to shake her paw and accept the pinecone.

"Shelby," he whispered, "you are such a beautiful soul." He gave her a big hug.

As he straightened up, Maurice playfully tapped Shelby's nose before tucking the pinecone in his jacket pocket.

"Well Caroline, looks like it's time to hit the road. I'm not going to say goodbye though, it sounds so permanent. But I will take a hug."

Maurice and I shared a long embrace. He noticed I was close to tears when we parted, so he gave me a kiss on the cheek.

I walked him to the Range Rover in silence. He climbed in the passenger seat and I wiped away a few tears. Gordon started the ignition and Maurice rolled down the window, leaned out to wave, and smiled his brilliant smile.

"See ya, Caroline," said Maurice.

"See ya, Mo."

Printed in Great Britain
by Amazon

23345702R00108